MW01097693

RESILIENT WARRIORS

An Anthology Composed

BY

SHANNON WHITTINGTON

CLC Publishing

Resilient Warriors

Printed in the United States of America

Introduction by Shannon Whittington
Forward by Rita Aragon

Book Design by Shannon Whittington
Cover Design by James Frazier, Frazier Creative, LLC

ISBN: 978-1722434595

Non-Fiction/Military/Biography

Resilient Warriors

This book is dedicated to The 22.

Each day, 22 veterans choose suicide as their way out. We must not stop reaching out, until that number changes from 22 to Zero.

Resilient Warriors

Contents

Resilient Warriors

ACKNOWLEDGMENTS

This book would not be possible without the help and cooperation of many individuals.

I would like to thank the 22 women who have faithfully served, or are serving, in our United States Armed Forces. Many of you stepped way outside your comfort zone in order to participate in this book. Your stories are incredible! Your selflessness continues in your service through the act of sharing your story. You will save someone through this process. Each one of you has my utmost respect – and my deepest gratitude.

I would like to thank the Books By Vets, Inc. board members. You all pushed me and kept me going through this project. There were times I wasn't sure it was going to come to fruition – you wouldn't let me stop. You connected me with many of the veterans in this book; you offered your help in editing the book; you kept me focused on our deadline and we made it!! Travis Johnson, Airial Dandridge, Donna Miller and Blythe Donovan – you all make our organization what it is. Thank you for seeing my vision and helping to make it even brighter!

I would like to thank the volunteers who helped with the editing of the book. Travis Johnson, Juli Wegner, Blythe Donovan, Matthew Whittington, and Bill Lloyd. Without your help, we would not have met the deadline.

I would like to thank our cover designer, James Frazier with Frazier Creative. Thank you for understanding our vision and purpose, and creating a cover that so beautifully exemplifies resiliency and captures the essences of our female warriors.

Last, but certainly not least, I would like to thank my husband, Matt Whittington. You are my everything, and without you, NONE of this would be possible.

INTRODUCTION

After founding the non-profit, Books By Vets, Inc., it was determined that we would do one anthology per year. The intent behind these books is to give veterans an opportunity to share their story. To give them a voice. And, ultimately, to give them their chance to once and for all share those parts of their story they tend to keep to themselves.

You see, when we keep our stories to ourselves, they have the ability to eat away at us to the point of complete destruction. Often, veterans reach this point and feel they have nowhere to turn. Life overcomes them. It all becomes too overwhelming, and sadly, suicide suddenly seems like the only way out.

We at Books By Vets, Inc. are incredibly fortunate to gain the trust of these veterans. To become an outlet for them. To offer a safe way for them to finally give purpose to their pain.

The women in this book didn't just write for themselves. They wrote for all the other veterans who are still suffering and wondering if it will ever get better. They wrote to empower other veterans to stand up and speak out. They wrote to leave a legacy.

Women have a very unique experience in the military. It's been a long fight for them to find their place – and after reading this book, you will learn that the fight isn't even close to over. Yet, they don't stop. They will not be stopped. They are soldiers. They are heroes. They are warriors. They are resilient.

Thank you for reading ~
Shannon Whittington

Resilient Warriors

FORWARD

Resiliency is not a new term or concept for the members of our nation's fighting forces. It is a new way of addressing how to prepare for the things that face defenders of freedom and those who are first responders. While the public is exposed to violence and its aftermath on screen and television, being face to face with the terrors of ripped and rendered flesh is distinctly different. Life in today's society is far from the days when pillaging and plundering of towns and villages wrought the spoils of conquering new territories; or is it?

We, as American service men and women, are not conquering nations to spread our own borders, but attempting to bring down despots and villainous dictators. Unfortunately, the experience for those on the ground may be very similar. These experiences make returning to American society a strange and foreign thing for our military brothers and sisters.

This book will share stories of female veterans who have faced challenges in their service to our nation and lived to return to families and communities that are foreign to their lives in service. This can cause some extreme reactions to those around them and can cause serious readjustment periods.

I joined the Air National Guard in 1979 and was part of a very small contingent, about 2%, of our fighting force, and juggled being a mother, teacher, and community member for 18 years. In order to achieve the rank of Colonel I had to take an active duty tour. With my children grown and gone from home, I signed on to full-time service just before 9/11. It was a time of pride and glory, and a time of loss and dismay, as Americans returned home broken or dead.

The changes our society had made were far different

from those soldiers returning from Vietnam, but for those involved in the horrors of war, their experiences were similar in their response to returning home.

Our nation loves her warriors, but not nearly enough is being done to restore the broken to full mental and physical health. It isn't that our nation is not moved by the broken, but so often the military members are not understood. How could they understand if you have not faced down the enemy and made life altering decisions based on your training?

I hope these stories of resilient women will be a source of pride and support for those who wrote them and for those reading them. Every day we make conscious decisions, let every day be a movement to lend support and strength to those who have served and continue to service the cause of liberty and justice.

Rita Aragon, Maj Gen (ret)
USAF

Resilient Warriors

AMBER NELSON, PV2
UNITED STATES ARMY

The thing you don't know (and cannot prepare for) when you make the decision to serve in the armed forces is the depth to which that decision is going to change who you are – not simply how you believe, how you feel, how you look, how you behave... but WHO YOU ARE. Once you make the decision and sign on the dotted line, once you traverse the initial training, you are forever, wholeheartedly, irrevocably indoctrinated. Like a mother bear of her cub, there is not a single thing you wouldn't do for her – for love of this incredibly amazing country we live in.

When I was young, I was in a very big hurry to make my mark on the world. I graduated from high school a bit early and joined the armed forces when I was still seventeen. I spent my eighteenth birthday in Fort Lewis, Missouri – Boot Camp. To this day, I have never done as many sets of 18 push-ups as I did that cold February day!

The Army was absolute culture shock. I recall landing at the airport and being collected at the gate by two men in Class-A dress uniforms. I expected to be yelled at from the moment I disembarked the airplane but was surprised how cordial they were. They escorted us through the airport and onto a commuter bus, destination: Reception Battalion- the 'in between' where the Army 'prepares' you for what comes next. I kept waiting for the yelling and pushups to start, as I had been warned by several friends about how things would be once I landed and was in the custody of the Army... but that yelling and drilling never happened during Reception... they kept us all in anticipation of when that 'other shoe would drop'.

It felt as if I spent that entire week at Reception Battalion standing in line! Stand in this line to be issued your uniforms, in this other line to be issued your field gear. Stand in this line to have your picture taken, and then go stand in that line to get some chow. I recall the first time I felt that I felt like I wasn't my own person anymore was standing in line for immunizations. I was issued a bright yellow immunization card and corralled into a single file line behind several other recruits. I was instructed to remove my long sleeve shirt and roll up the sleeves of my t-shirt on both sides. When I took my next step forward, a person on my right and one on my left put a 'gun' containing an injection/immunization to each arm and pulled the trigger. I flinched, then heard an ominous voice say, "step forward private". I took another step forward and was injected again. One more step and the soldier with the needle grabbed wrist and pulled my forearm into view - I was injected under the skin – a TB test... one more step and I was provided a gauze pad and two Band aids. I looked at my arms and noticed blood running down each arm that I quickly wiped away and covered as I was being herded to the next line. That moment gave me a glimpse of what was to come. It occurred to me that I was just a number right then... no longer my own person, and not yet a soldier. I recall being issued a small book of Army Regulations that I was expected to know – my "new bible", and I recall several classes during that week geared to point out all of the different parts of those Army Regulations that we were all expected to understand and abide.

On the day we were sent to our units – the day boot camp actually began, any niceties we had experienced to that point came to an abrupt halt! Drill Sergeants playing metal trashcan lids like cymbals awakened us that morning. It was absolute chaos – crashing of the trashcan lids and yelling for us to do things we hadn't yet been taught to do. We stumbled out of bed unsure of what was going on and did our best to comply with what we were being asked to do. Looking back now, there are several moments of my experiences that I wish I had video footage of... this is one of those moments... the confusion was intense (although, I am sure it would be the same confusion and chaos to be awoken from a dead sleep in the middle of the night to sirens alerting soldiers to inbound missiles) ... food for thought – a really great reason to start the training out in this way. These unexpected chaotic wake ups happened periodically during boot camp. They became very manageable and much less chaotic as time progressed.

We dressed and gathered our belongings under this duress. Imagine this for a moment. Somewhere around 120 of us... I am 5'4" and at this point weigh about 114 pounds. My 'Belongings' now consist of everything I came here with (which was one duffel bag) and now EVERYTHING that the Army just issued me – a duffel bag (so big that I could climb into it) packed to overflowing with uniforms and gear, plus my rucksack also packed to the brim with gear. Each of us struggling to carry everything we own, we were herded like cattle into the back of an actual cattle trailer (you know, the aluminum semi-trailers with breathing holes) being pulled by a semi. There was not a place to sit, and even if there were, there would not have been room so we each did the best we could to support each other to keep our belongings in hand and stay standing so as not to be trampled by those around us trying to do the same. The ride was terribly disorienting, as you could not tell where we were going.

When the semi stopped, the end of the cattle trailer opened downward to create a ramp. There were three Drill Sergeants in battle dress uniform and funny 'Smokey the Bear' hats standing there to greet a silent trailer full of would be soldiers.

That is when the true chaos began- our morning didn't hold a candle to what was happening now. From this point on, everything occurred with a sense of urgency and it was understood that the expectation was for you to do it perfectly, even if you didn't fully understand what it was that was being asked of you.

'Shakedown'

We were herded to a large open room and lined up with all of our belongings. We were given seconds to remove the content of all of our bags on the ground for "inspection". The Drill Sergeants would walk from person to person and find things to yell at them for – I think the point was to make sure everyone knew that nobody was special- nobody was top of the class – everybody was doing everything wrong... but those Drill Sergeants were going to fix all of that by showing us the military way (the right way).

I have always been pretty empathic – able to tell a kind soul despite the outward appearance. My drill Sergeant had a kind face and I felt, a kind heart. The kind of person you look at and just expect a warm interaction. He was doing a fabulous job playing the part of rough and tough drill instructor- the "fear me, respect me" role. I have NO IDEA what came over me in that moment but watching this drill instructor pretend to be so mean while my instincts told me he was kind struck me funny and I laughed a little out loud. I don't recommend that!

He saw me giggle and I became an instant target – he walked up to me and got right in my face – he asked me what I thought was so funny to which I replied "nothing" as I glanced at my feet... it didn't end there – not by a long shot. "Look at me when I talk to you soldier" ... "What are you staring at? Are you eyeballing me Private?" There was no way to get out of this situation except learn the lesson that was being taught. Ultimately, he made everyone else do pushups while I stood up and watched them because he said, "This private feels that she is better than everyone else!" That was the last time I stepped out of turn during boot camp. I was the first person in my platoon to cause everyone else to suffer and I learned that moment how important my focus was.

Six weeks after my boot camp birthday, I was off to Redstone Arsenal, Alabama for advance individual training in my specialty.

My MOS (or Military Occupational Specialty) was Ammunition Specialist. This designation made me responsible for ordering, receiving, transporting, and safely storing all manner of ordnance; supplying ordnance as required, and for safely and effectively receiving and decommissioning unexploded ordnance as necessary. My training was intensive. I excelled at it and enjoyed my job entirely.

In early 1994 the US military began deploying what would turn out to be some 20,000 troops to intervene and aid in restoring democracy in Haiti following the overthrow of the recently elected Democratic President by a Haitian military coup occurring in 1991. Shortly after arriving to my duty station in Fort Hood, Texas my battalion began receiving orders and shipping out to Guantanamo Bay Naval Base to lend support.

The same week that my unit began receiving orders, I came down with what I initially thought was food poisoning. After a few days of persistent symptoms, I went to see the doctor. I learned that I was approximately 6 weeks pregnant. That little lab slip changed the trajectory of my life in one single day (*Company Halt! About Face!*) I always knew I wanted to be a parent one day, but I imagined that I would plan it with a mate and that I would be a bit older before it happened.

The same day I learned of my pregnancy, my Master Sergeant removed me from my potentially hazardous duties in the field and put me on a desk job at company headquarters "per Army Regulation". I understood the rationale for this decision, but it was difficult not to feel like I was letting my team down somehow. My pregnancy was accidental and unexpected, but I was restricted from performing the hazardous duties for which my MOS demanded simply due to the condition I found myself in while my teammates were still in the field. I recall a male Specialist that I worked with who was struggling with Army life. He regularly spoke of wishing he could "get the hell out of here". When he learned that I had been transferred to a desk job and why he looked at me with an expression I have yet to identify and said, "must be nice – just get yourself knocked up and voilà – get out of jail free card". His words still elicit negative feelings for me – shame, I think mostly. I spent the rest of my time on active duty wondering if everyone I met was thinking the same thing.

As my battalion dwindled and my pregnancy progressed, the reality settled in that I would soon be solely responsible for another human life. I realized how unprepared I was for what was to come. I mean, I had a basic clue about how to be a mom - I was fairly confident that I could keep a child fed, clean and warm... and I already loved her beyond measure. I knew how to be a soldier -it's pretty straightforward – you display integrity and you follow orders. It occurred to me though, that I had NO IDEA how to accomplish the task of doing both at the same time, as both would require 100% of me. I suppose it was my young age and relative immaturity that made me think that the Army would have a plan for me to follow in this instance... some way for me to have my cake and eat it too. *They must have dealt with this before... right? Women soldiers get pregnant all of the time.*

The answer I sought was not forthcoming. I was made aware that as I was a single, unwed soldier, and the child's father was not involved, my options were limited. As soon as the child was born, and I was cleared for duty, I would be deployed and would need to make arrangements with "someone you trust – your parents or grandparents perhaps" to retain custody of my child while I was away. I began to shake, as I was fiercely afraid in that moment. I realized THAT MOMENT that I was no longer a child. For several years prior to this, I had fancied myself quite mature– I thought that joining the Army among other "grown up" decisions I had made up until that point were evidence of this maturity. Standing there, I realized that I was a child and that the adult world was terrifying. I kept my composure as best I could muster and asked if there was an option B. My Master Sergeant told me that under the circumstances, I could choose to be honorably discharged under Chapter 8 – a medical discharge for pregnancy.

The next few days were THE most difficult days I had lived up until that point in my life. *I didn't plan this, but it happened, and I am in it alone. I already love this child beyond measure and there is no way that I can be convinced to abort or to give up. I want her. I love her. How do I make a unilateral decision to keep this baby and then ask my parents to raise her while I go attend to my duties as a soldier? Of course they would say yes, but it is not right to make that decision for them – they didn't ask for this! If I am choosing to keep her - to be a mom, is it right that I would deliver her and then simply leave for an unknown amount of time – would she even know me when I returned? What about my oath? I made a promise to this country... and it is my child's country... would it not be an act of love to continue to defend it for my child? Being a soldier is how I make a living... how will I make a living if I leave the Army?*

It is hard for me to reconcile my actual time in service with the affect that brief time had on my psyche. Even as I write this chapter, I find myself uncovering and confronting feelings and emotions that I thought were put to rest long ago. I enlisted in the United States Army and signed on for a three-year tour on active duty. Though my discharge was honorable, I was unable to complete my tour of duty- a truth that has never set well with me. In my heart, I serve this country still today.

Joining the military was the best decision I had made in my life up until that point. It was the first productive 'grown-up' decision I had made, and the things that I learned in the military set me up well for the life I have ultimately led. My time in the Army was short but impactful- changing me at my core and preparing me for adulthood in ways I couldn't have imagined. The training pushed my physical and emotional limits well beyond what I thought I was capable of and showed me just how far I could go without breaking.

I played volleyball in middle school and high school, but nobody would ever describe me as that 'athletic type'. I enjoyed music classes and the arts... though I always admired those athletic friends, I did not enjoy physical education at all! I recall an early morning in Alabama – the whole base was running that morning, though I don't recall the reason. My platoon ran 6 miles in 45 minutes and all of us stayed in formation for the entire run. I am sure that there are many who will read this and think this feat trivial – but it was a big deal for me as it changed the way I viewed my physical limits from that day on... it would be fair to say it removed my brain from the equation and showed me that I can go as far physically as I need to, whenever I need to. The feeling I had that morning when our 6 miles was done is a feeling that has stuck with me for my whole life. I have recalled those moments just after completing that run many times in my life when I have run into moments when I felt like I could not go on, and I have always gone on... and made it to the other side of whatever the obstacle relatively unscathed!

My job in the Army was dangerous if not done with care. I learned how incredibly important true teamwork and camaraderie was... my life would literally be in their hands and theirs in mine. I recall being acutely aware of the recruits that I would hesitate to trust with my life; and I remember the gravity of the moment it occurred to me (like a sledgehammer to my gut) that I could not allow myself to become 'that soldier', the one that could not be trusted, that I had to become the soldier anyone would feel at ease going into battle with. I had to strive for excellence. I had to understand everything about my job- how to do it right, how to do it safely. I understood how important it was to avoid cutting corners or, pardon, 'half-ass' the job. This too has spilled over into my life since the military. As it were, I was destined to work in the medical field. This early understanding of how important it is to get it right has stayed with me for all of these years since leaving the military and has served me well in my profession. "Attention to detail!" ...Not simply something the Drill Sergeant yells at you while pulling apart your locker, examining your wardrobe, or quality checking your ability to field strip and reassemble your weapon – but an invaluable set point for the way a soldier approaches everything in life.

Although I know, in retrospect, that my decision to leave the military when I did was the right one. I do find myself shying away from conversations about my having been in the military and I do not always volunteer that I am a veteran. For this very reason, I almost declined to write this chapter. Whenever I find myself in a conversation about my veteran status, I fear the questions that always follow – particularly, "how long did you serve?". In truth, I am still ashamed of not having completed the full tour I signed up for. I feel I got so much more than I gave. I learned so very much from the Army about the kind of person I want to be. I feel so fortunate to have had the opportunity to be a soldier - the lessons I learned during my service have never left me.

It is difficult to have so much appreciation for the experience but still have regrets. In committing all of this to paper, I find myself questioning if I would have done things differently given the chance. I absolutely would not. My experience has led me to where I am now, and I recognize that any changes to that road may not have led me to this place!

ARTHALIA WEEKES
UNITED STATES ARMY

I would like to say that I always thought that I would have joined the Army; but in looking back over my life I think it was more of a push from where I was, just so I could "get out" of what I was in. I entered the military as a scrawny young woman, age 21 from Macon, Georgia. I did not have the greatest life growing up, but I knew that I wanted more than what I was currently getting. The reality was that I was afraid of getting stuck and becoming another statistic of "something started but never finished". So, I joined with no questions and to much of the surprise of my family; the United States Army-Be all I can Be! I was told so many things to keep me in Macon, but I had made up my mind that nothing could change my life from what it was except the military. I joined and went through Basic Training. It was fun, challenging, and scary at times. But I made it through. I think it was at that moment that I began to realize that I had something to prove, that I could make it; that I was not my life circumstances.

There were so many things I was exposed to in Basic alone that shifted my view on what adulting looked like, or how it even felt. I wasn't good at sit-ups, even though I was tiny. I ran and passed, but it was a struggle. Being a leader was where I shined and thrived. I can remember being shown pictures of Desert Storm by a drill sergeant. I told my battle buddies, who were crying and afraid, to suck it up. This is what we signed up for. I didn't think we were going to war for real; I didn't see the future of Iraq or Afghanistan on the horizon. Nevertheless, I wanted to represent all that a hoo-ah solider was. I wasn't the best athlete in the military, but I was a great soldier who excelled in everything else expected of me. I proved to my family that the little girl they knew growing up was not that girl anymore; but a grown woman who endured the toughest of training and who would stick it out until she retired, whatever that entailed. When I failed at something, it was an issue for me because it went against all I was trying to prove. Everything that counted me out - my past, my lack of finishing college - the Army changed all that for me.

Here is a small side bar: I realize even now, many people do not have this warm and fuzzy view of the military and the impact the experience has had on them. A lot of it quite honestly is probably negative, especially being a woman in the military and, quite frankly, being an African American woman in the military. I had to rely on my intelligence to be accepted and to impact others. I had to prove that I was not this hood chick that was always angry and upset. Everything I did was ridiculed. Even if my response was a mature one as not to end someone else's career. I had to fight for position, for respect, for my character just because of this factor alone. Yet it did not change my view or hope that this mandate I was given, that was destined to push me forward in my life, so I would never have to prove something again. Now don't get it twisted; I had skill and still do, but there was this emotional piece within me that I truly believe the military brought out. I discovered the person - good, bad, ugly and indifferent.

Acceptance is a hard deal when you are so super strong. I laugh at myself because there was always this desire to have this persona of strength. A lot of times I felt weak because of something I did not do, did not excel at or was not received by others in the ranks; nevertheless, I pushed forward. However, there was this time that while serving I encountered what I thought would have never happened to me. I knew how to handle myself; I didn't need anyone fighting my battles for me; I could do it myself. I can remember sitting on the steps of the building in which I worked. This civilian man was always looking at me strange, but I ignored it and chocked it up as creepy. He was a retired Command Sergeant Major (CSM) and was the chief in one of the sections in the building. He came to me and made an offer I declined. He continued to press as I continued to become more irate in my response. I was cornered with this oversized man looking at me; telling me all the things he could do for me and to me. I could handle him, I said in my mind, and I did just that without hesitation and he finally gave up. I decided that it was not a big deal but had shared it with a co-worker who in turn shared it with my civilian boss, a retired First Sergeant (1SG). I could not tell you how I arrived at this place, but I was on the Sergeant Major's red carpet at parade rest for putting this man in his place. I was reprimanded for his actions, even though I had thought to handle it at the lowest level. Heck, I thought he was just some nasty old civilian that I had simply put in his place. But my boss did not see it that way, he said that I should have told him, and he no longer wanted me in his section, since I did not trust him. Nothing happened to the man that harassed me. But me? I was given the lowest Non-Commissioned Officer Evaluation Report that I had ever received since becoming a Non-Commissioned Officer and transferred to another section.

I think what got to me most was that my Sergeant Major was a female, and, in my mind, she should have stood up for me or addressed it differently. But she became one of those people in my life that disappointed me, let me down, saddened me, hurt me, used me, ridiculed me; all in one action. I always felt that this didn't sound like much of a big deal. I knew that there were so many female veterans, and even active duty females, who have encountered sexual harassment to the point of an assault. I minimized the impact this had on me; but it left a bitter taste in my mouth towards the military and more specifically towards its leadership. I was a Non-Commissioned Officer, no one was more professional than I, a leader of soldiers. I prided myself on this. But the very thing that got me out of the life I was in, became the very thing that looked like my old life. Even in that, I said to myself, "Lesson learned. I can still be great, this will pass, too." My faith carried me, but I did not quite heal from it. Rather, I hid from it and consumed myself in work once more.

I "enjoyed" life, trained the soldiers and all that jazz. It was lovely. No one had to know that I was simply hurt by this pattern set in my life. I ran away from it back in Macon, just to run right back into it in the military. I experienced loss from those who touched my life in ways that still resonate with me. Yet, I numbed myself from so much, that I was disconnected. I made stupid decisions within my personal life that made me question my own character, or what type of aroma I was giving off for someone to even be okay with approaching me the way they did at times. I lost myself in the essence of it all. Not just because of the sexual harassment, but because of the disappointment within myself. I came here to free myself, and instead I was sabotaging myself. I stayed on the surface of things and not even my closest friends could penetrate the wall that I had built up. I still did my job well, but I also developed this "I do not care" attitude.

My first marriage ended, but I was okay with that although I had said I would never get a divorce. A man and his family that spoke into me, in all my disarray, saw past that mess and took me in. When I received the call at work from someone trying to verify his death, I was shaking. In all my life, he was the one along with his family, that saw beyond what I tried to show and accepted me anyway. He was the epitome of a leader in the military who didn't taint the word or the role and now he was no longer here. I regretted that I didn't reach out more, but somehow, I'm at peace, and knew even that wasn't held against me.

I experienced loss, more heartache and I simply continued to hide in it while still excelling in my career. I said earlier how my faith carried me, and it did in a lot of ways. There was a point where I turned away from it with my hands up, but God still showed me grace. He covered me and captured me with his love. Yet, I did not know how to receive that love, explain it, or even what to do with it. But he kept giving it to me through others who were genuine, through signs of the times, and yes even in my career.

I can't say I ever truly trusted leadership the same way again. What I can say, is that I opened more to the idea of doing so because of the people who crossed my path. A lot of days I wonder what would have happened had I stayed in the Army, had I reported that nasty old man, had I stood up more to the female Sergeant Major, had I said no, had I realized that I had lost something within. Would I have addressed it sooner? Would I have these amazing set of friends? Or, would I have retired like I always wanted to? I am not sure. I cannot continue to let my past define who I am destined to be, and what I am destined to change into.

I used to say all the time that it is not easy being green. I took that from Kermit the Frog because he was dating a pig that in no way he could ever procreate with, but somehow against all odds, despite the oddness in it, he and Ms. Piggy made it work. I tell myself I can no longer ignore the impact of my experiences in the military. Here I have only touched the surface. Truth be told, it was not all bad, but it was not all good. I faced so much in my personal life while trying to lead soldiers who were facing their own personal issues.

I have dedicated my life beyond the military to be the voice for those who can't say it out loud or who have not said it out loud. I work with Veterans on a daily basis and it is pure in its purest form of what can happen when we hide within. That pureness is not clean, it's real. It's what we are afraid to show others. It's a place where we feel like we are in it alone and no one understands where we are coming from. I can say that I find myself in this place; but I make the effort to rise above, even if it is just a little bit. My destiny has not changed because of what I went through. My destiny can still be fulfilled *because* I went through it and because I am still here standing, working and not hiding.

I know it may seem like I am all over the place, and that my story is not a story to tell at all. To a degree I may incline myself to agree with you. Instead, let's look at this as a message of hope, of expectancy, of reminder, of thought, of will, of mind, and of emotion. That no matter the story, no matter the experience, there is something to be gathered and reflected upon to push you into change.

I don't know what your life has been like. I know that to tell your story in some way is the first step to healing. That what you went through is not mediocre, that it meant something, it was real. We can choose at times to hide in our pain and think we are living life like it's golden.

In actuality we are existing and surviving another day. Healing does not come when we keep our mouths closed or not let those tears fall. We cannot continue to hold up within ourselves and think things will automatically shift for us and then we are good. We have to move, we have to communicate, we have to do something that will evoke a change within. Strength is not defined by how much muscle you have, or how much you put others in their place, or all those joyful posts you post. Strength shines through in our honesty within ourselves first, and being real about it. I don't have it all together. There are times when I am just done with things and want to quit. That's real life, that's the adulting lesson I have learned. Each day I realize that my role in the military, the events I experienced, (wanted or not) have helped to shape me in some way - destined me to change!

I have seen myself alone in a room full of people, but today as I write; the room is filling which means there is a place for hope.

BARBARA TURNER, LT
UNITED STATES NAVY

Naval Air Station Pensacola
National Museum of Naval Aviation
Blue Angel Atrium
Friday, 1 November 1996

I retired today as a 42-year old Navy Lieutenant with twenty-two years of honorable naval service. How did I arrive at this place, at this time? I enlisted in the Navy and climbed the enlisted ranks from Seaman Recruit (E-1) to Aviation Maintenance Administrationman (AZ) Senior Chief (E-8) before I was commissioned a naval officer (Ensign 01E) via the Limited Duty Officer (LDO) Program. I was designated an enlisted Helicopter Naval Aircrewman while assigned to Helicopter Training Squadron EIGHTEEN (HT-18) in February 1976 as an Airman (E-3). As a Detachment Aviation Maintenance Officer during my tour in Helicopter Combat Support Squadron SIX (HC-6), along with two CH-46 Sea Knight helicopters, six pilots, a Chief and approximately 25 E-6 and below personnel, we deployed to the Mediterranean Sea onboard the USS Butte (AE-27) for seven months, and more. Somewhere in the middle of these two duty stations I managed to fall in love with, and marry, a sailor in Sicily and together we had three wonderful sons all while we were both on active duty in the Navy! It was a wonderful life that I would not trade for anything else in the world!

My parents, Bob and Betty Couch, are seated on the front row next to my husband ABHC Ben Turner, USN (Retired) and our three sons, J. R., Mike and T.J. They are here to watch and take part in my retirement ceremony. My parents kept every letter, every card, every evaluation, award and promotion that I mailed home during my career and they brought everything to me today as I retired twenty-two years later. Among several friends and colleagues in attendance today are my boot camp Company Commander, DPCS Jouay Koppari, USN (Retired), a former Division Officer LCDR William "Tuck" Edwards, USN (Retired) and his wife Ann, who drove over from Panama City, FL. and retired Master Chief Yeoman (YNCM) Kathy Seader, USN (Retired) who drove up from Orlando, FL. One of my very best friends and "buddy" who joined the Navy with me, Karen (Meek) Lyming and her mom were there too. My closest and very best friend, AZC Kathy Hall, USN (Retired) rounded out my VIPs.

My troops are here too, but they are not standing in formation behind the seating reserved for guests; they are sitting with everyone else. Having stood in formation a time or two myself for inspections, retirement and change of command ceremonies, I thought it would be a nice change to have my troops sit among my family and friends. Having served as an enlisted sailor for sixteen years, I could appreciate the importance of this small gesture and always made taking care of my enlisted sailors my priority.

I was the Assistant Director for the Aviation Water Survival Department, Naval Aviation Schools Command (NASC), Naval Air Station (NAS) Pensacola (FL) when I retired. Morning Quarters were held at 0800 to allow me to say "thank you and goodbye" to my sailors. All decked out in their service dress blue uniforms and assembled in the gym for inspection, I had the privilege of walking up and down the ranks to look each one in the eye, shake their hand and pass on my appreciation for jobs well done.

How many military retirement ceremonies, Navy personnel inspections and change of command ceremonies have I attended these past twenty-two years? How many friends and colleagues have I witnessed retire as I stood in formation? How many of these ceremonies have taken place in this National Museum of Naval Aviation? Too many to remember. As I sit on the Dais on such a beautiful fall day in the Blue Angel Atrium, retiring from the United States Navy that I have given my life, my heart and my soul to for so many years, I remember back to the first time I was in this very Museum......

I was born in Garden City, Kansas in 1954 and grew up in a two-bedroom, one-bathroom house on 7th street. It was a great neighborhood with lots of kids. Mostly boys though. Probably why I was a tom boy right from the start. We moved to Topeka (KS) in 1968 and I graduated from Topeka High School in 1972.

Why did I enlist in the Navy? Because I was bored as hell and going nowhere fast! I was engaged to be married a year after I graduated from high school and I did attend Washburn University for one entire semester ... oh my God, that was painful. I wasn't ready to go to college and I certainly wasn't ready to become a wife at 18. My engagement was called off (best decision ever) and as I read all the mail from my brother, who enlisted in the Navy in 1969, I thought his letters were so amazing and reading about where he was, so exciting. I remember when he called home one time at 4:00 AM and when I answered the phone, he said, *"Hey sis, what'cha doing?"* and I said, *"Sleeping stupid, what are you doing?"* He was calling from Japan! I thought it sounded like a lot of fun, so having no interest in college, and not much interest in hanging out waiting for something else to come along, I enlisted.

I went to see the recruiters and I remember standing in the entryway and looking at how each door was "decorated" with respective service logos and posters and pictures of the soldiers, sailors, airmen, and Marines and thinking to myself, how would I look in those uniforms? Crazy, right?

Not really. I thought that joining the Navy WAVES (**W**omen **A**ccepted for **V**olunteer **E**mergency **S**ervice) sounded sexy and I loved the cracker jacks that the sailors wore, too. I didn't particularly care for the Army or the Marine Corps uniform because, quite frankly their uniforms were a bit too drab for me and not much creation went toward their uniform design (in my opinion) and the Air Force blue wasn't a good fit, either. Navy wins! When I sat down to dinner that night with mom and dad I made the announcement that I had enlisted in the Navy for three years. There wasn't much of a reaction from my mom and dad right away, but believe me, I had reaction later! They both stopped eating and looked at each other with sad eyes, as if to say, "*Now Barbie will be gone too.*"

My mom worked in a large bank along with my friend Karen's mother. Karen was one year behind me in high school and wasn't doing anything either. When my mom went to work the next day, she told Karen's mom all about my enlisting. The phone rang shortly after Karen found out about my plans and I got her hooked up with my recruiter. We ended up joining the Navy on the Buddy Program, which guaranteed us the same duty station right after we graduated from boot camp.

OATH OF ENLISTMENT

Raise your right hand and repeat after me: "*I, Barbara Louise Couch, do solemnly swear that I will support and defend the Constitution of the United States against all enemies, foreign and domestic; that I will bear true faith and allegiance to the same; and that I will obey the orders of the President of the United States and the orders of the officers appointed over me, according to regulations and the Uniform Code of Military Justice. So help me God!*"

Friday, 8 November 1974 – United States Navy or Bust

There we were at the Kansas City, MO airport waiting to board an airplane that would take us to Orlando, Florida. The three of us: Karen,
Eileen and myself were all from Kansas and on our way to Navy boot camp in Orlando, home of Disney World. Wow! We were excited and nervous all at the same time.

We said our goodbyes to our families and boarded the plane. When we arrived at the Orlando airport, we were told to "muster" (what the heck does that mean?) outside where a Navy bus would take us to the base. So, we grabbed our luggage and went outside to find a Navy Petty Officer with a clipboard, standing beside a Navy-blue bus. He was very nice and checked our names off his list as we got on the bus. We were all chatting and introducing ourselves to each other and then as we got closer to the base we became quiet and somber. It was too late to turn back now.

It was late at night when we finally arrived on the base and we were told to "fall in" (do what?) on the sidewalk. Then the fun began, and the very nice Petty Officer started yelling at us right away and I thought that he needed to relax...we weren't going anywhere. We got in to three lines and stood at some form of attention. When the luggage was taken off the bus, we identified our own and picked it up to go in to what would become our home for the next nine weeks.

We had to go up three flights of stairs to get to our barracks and we would soon learn that stairs didn't exist anymore; they were called ladders. Funniest looking ladder I had ever seen ~ look Ma no rungs! Once inside our barracks, we were greeted by a Company Commander (CC) and she was yelling at us, too! Boy, they sure were a grouchy bunch. We had to "hit the line" and shut up! We all sort of stood there looking at each other wondering what "hit the line" meant. We soon found out that it meant we all had to stand at attention, lined up facing inward toward each other, and our toes could not go over this certain line in the tile. Good grief. It was late, and we were tired and just wanted to go to bed.

There were seventy-two women in Company 3170 from all walks of life and we were to learn to work as a team and become U.S. Navy WAVES; to transition from civilian to sailor in nine weeks! Our Company Commander (CC) was Data Processing Technician Second Class Petty Officer, Jouay Koppari and I was impressed with her and wanted to be just like her. She was so squared away and sharp, and I knew I would learn a lot from her. Yes, joining the Navy was the right choice after all.

My first letter home five days after arrival.

13 November 1974

SR Barbara Couch SSN (yes, we actually had to include our SSN in our address)
Naval Training Center – 3170
Orlando, Florida 32893

"Dad & Mom –
This is our 1 – 3 day and so far, it's okay I guess. We got our uniforms yesterday and had to wash & dry & iron one white shirt, one blue pair of slacks and our hats & ties. We had to gang iron them, which meant that there were five ironing boards with three girls ironing (all) shirts and 4 girls ironing slacks and 3 ironing caps. That put 2 people on one ironing

board. We have to wash & iron uniforms every night. (What a huge pain that was).

*The CC made me cadence caller yesterday and today I am turning it over to someone else because everyone takes smaller steps, and everyone is supposed to take a 24" step while marching which is the same way we were taught in Drill Team. I cried today because everyone was complaining, and I told the MAA (master at arms) that she could shove it. The 1st platoon is always out of step with the 2nd platoon and the RCPO (**R**ecruit **C**hief **P**etty **O**fficer) (a real bitch!) keeps getting out of step, too, and then she yells at me to get in step. She makes me sick.*

I am a little homesick and I have bad news. We must be here __11__ weeks instead of __9__ weeks because of x-mas. If nobody goes home for the 2 weeks that we get off for x-mas, then we can graduate in 9 weeks. But there are already three girls who are going home for those two weeks. So that means they will lose their two weeks leave after boot camp – they will have to go straight to their "A" school. So, the ones who don't go home during x-mas will just be here – we can't move up or graduate until everyone is here. We will still get our 2 weeks leave though after boot. Oh! Also, Karen & I have both put in for the RAP program. That means Recruit Assistance Program right after boot camp, we can go home and work at the recruiters' office for 10 days with $25 a day additional to our base pay. NEAT. Then we have our 2 weeks leave.

We just came back from chow (lunch) and the food is getting better I guess. We now have a new RCPO – she ought to do better.

I have quit smoking because of my cold. We got a penicillin shot yesterday and another shot today. We also had blood taken out. The only time my arms hurt is when someone touches me there. I'm bunking on top and Humphrey is bunking below. She's from Ohio; all or most of the group seems to be getting along well.

My graduation (now) should be Jan 24, 1975 but I'll have to let you know for sure. Well not much else. Oh! We get our pictures taken for our ID card only today. When we get our dress uniforms, I'll send you a picture.

We went swimming Monday morning and I classified for a 3rd class swimmer (that's the highest) we had to float for 5 minutes and then swim 50 yards (150 ft), which is a heck of a long way. Well, gotta go. (WRITE SOON)

P. S. I think that the CC is gonna make me 5th squad leader which makes me cool. And I'll get to be a 1st class petty officer recruit. Bye again, Love Barb"

My parents received a FORM letter from the Commanding Officer of Recruit Training Command (RTC) Orlando **dated 19 November 1974** with six pages of frequently asked questions and answers. <u>One question and answer are very important to explain here</u>.

Q. *"How can recruits be contacted while undergoing training?"*
A. <u>BY MAIL</u>. *"In order that your recruit may receive mail with the least possible delay, please use the following address."* The letter went on to say, *"The first few weeks are rigorous, and your recruit may not have the time to write home as frequently as desired. Please be patient in awaiting the first mail."*

The reason that I point out this particular question/answer is because my parents had not received any mail from me and were getting very concerned. It had only been eleven days and we had not been allowed to call home yet and they were pretty upset. Letter or not, my Dad (God love him) decided to call the Commanding Officer (CO) **of the base** to find out why they had not heard from their daughter! My first taste of how the chain-of-command works, from the top down, would soon be a huge learning experience for me.

I was called in to the CC's office to take a phone call. I, of course, had no idea that when I said, "*Seaman Recruit Couch speaking, sir*" that I would hear my Dad's voice on the line. I was shocked at first and then scared that something bad had happened. Then I found out that my dad had *convinced* the base CO that it would be in the CO's best interest if he could speak with me, **NOW**! We spoke briefly, and I explained that I was just fine and that I had mailed a couple of letters home and they should be receiving them any day now. (We were required to write at least one letter home each Sunday!)

Boy was I ever in deep trouble when I got off the phone! My CC (all five foot nothing – with folded arms) said something like "*I don't know who your Dad is, but ...*" I had to do extra calisthenics and clean the CC's office all by myself. Was she ever upset with me! (and that is putting it mildly) I never knew until much later that when the CO got the call from my Dad that he, the CO, had then called the Regimental Commander who in turn called the Battalion Commander, who then called my Company Commander. That is how I found out about shit rolling downhill with me at the bottom. As an aside, Mom told me that she and Dad had the discussion for a few days before he called the base and Mom tried to talk him out of calling because she knew that I would get in trouble. My Dad would have no part of that! His job at the time was Security and Exchange Corporation Commissioner for the State of Kansas. His job title (position) made him third in line to succeed the Kansas Governor, should the need arise. So, Dad had some power that he rarely used or felt the need to use it...except of course in this case!

One good thing that resulted from that phone call was that the Company were marched over to the Navy Exchange (the very next day) to do a little shopping and then PHONE HOME!! And that was an order! *Aye, aye ma'am*! Dad was very protective of his little girl and he was not a happy camper at all when he had not heard from me when he thought I should have written or been allowed to call home. My folks talked about that for several years and we always had a good laugh about it.

Every team needs good leaders and we went through two RCPO's in a little less than two weeks. I was trying to keep my head down and blend in with the rest of the Company, when one Friday afternoon all three of us Kansas girls were called in to the Lounge. The Lounge is where we were able to study, write letters home, or smoke when allowed and listen and dance to music on occasion. That is when we learned that our CC wasn't happy with how things were going, and we had just failed another inspection! That afternoon was when I was handed the RCPO collar device, Karen was handed the MAA (Master-At-Arms) collar device, and Eileen the Company Yeoman. Talk about being put in charge early on! Right after we were "pinned", our CC took her red Aiguillette (all CC's wore them to identify them as such) off and taped it to the Lounge window, and then she turned around and said to the Company *"I QUIT"*, and then she walked out! Just like that, she was gone! She left us with another CC who should have been a Marine Corps Drill Sergeant! She drilled us all weekend long and never let up! We were pooped and dirty and really wishing that our CC had never left. Yes, our CC did come back on

Monday morning, but made it seem that she only came back because we had finally decided to get our shit together as a Company. Boy were we ever happy to see her.

Every second of every minute of every hour of every day was scheduled for us and unless you were a complete idiot, you could get through boot camp without much trouble at all. Each of the, what turned out to be eleven weeks, or 77 days were identified as, for example 3 – 1 Day, which meant the third 3rd week and the 1st day of that week and we knew exactly what we would be doing each moment of those nine, or rather eleven, weeks. We were extended two weeks because in "their" infinite wisdom, "they, the powers that be" decided to allow half of the Company to go home on Christmas leave...ha! They knew not what they did, and I can tell you that it never happened again! All Companies were allowed the same opportunity, not just my Company. We graduated from Navy boot camp on Friday, January 17, 1975 and drove to Milton, FL with Karen's uncle Danny, an active duty Navy Lieutenant Commander.

Remember I said that I had been here before? In the National Museum of Naval Aviation?

Monday, 14 April 1975

I was a twenty-year-old Airman Apprentice (E-2) stationed in Helicopter Training Squadron EIGHTEEN (HT-18) at NAS Whiting Field, Milton, FL. Four short months after I reported to my helicopter squadron, the very first formal military ceremony that I participated in was onboard NAS Pensacola, FL. Phase 1 of the National Museum of Naval Aviation was dedicated that day and I, along with several hundred other military personnel, was in attendance. In fact, most of my squadron personnel were there. I was looking very sharp and squared away in my Summer Light Blue uniform and when I visually surveyed the people in attendance, all I saw was a sea of navy gold brass. I should have had on sunglasses with all that gold shining! I think that every available sailor from every command in the Pensacola area was there that day as each command "fell in" formation for the official ceremonies. It was an incredible day and so much happened like seeing and hearing the Navy Band from New Orleans and being part of the ceremony itself. I loved the precision of that ceremony! I loved the daily challenges that I faced, and I loved that I could do whatever I wanted to do if I chose to do it. I loved the Navy.

LT Barbara L. (Couch) Turner, USN (Retired)
8 November 1974 – 1 November 1996

BOBBI REED
UNITED STATES ARMY

Joining the Army as a Woman in 1973

It was the beginning of my last year of Bay Shore High School; it was September 1972 and next month I was turning 17. My life so far had been so very hard. Along with the various trying times being a teenager in the early 1970s, me growing up in an abusive household had been my greatest challenge up to this point. My father was a minister, so I grew up as a "PK", a preacher's kid. I had developed some "toughness" from these constant challenges as a teenager and beyond. I had to learn skills that some children never had to, but to this day am grateful for it.

My father was a loving, caring, kind-hearted person who would give you literally the shirt off of his back. He is remembered by many as being "the rock" during many challenging situations in their lives. As we suffered severe abuse (mental, emotional and physical) from mom, my dad struggled to get her to stop. Back in that day, divorce was not popular, especially with his position in the church. You pretended everything was okay and tried to survive the situation. Besides, mom hit and verbally abused him as well. I had run away 6-7 times already. I would get so overwhelmed with the arguments, the physical hurting, and the emotional pain that I would stay gone overnight; shacking up in my boyfriend's basement, unbeknownst to his parents.

Every time I did this, I always thought ahead to take a change of clothes and would attend school the next day. I think back now and think "how crazy I was" not to skip the school the next day. It was convenient that he lived right down the street from the school, but most kids in that time would have cut school. I was respectful of education, thinking that this would be my "ticket" to a good future along with a way out of my "hellhole". I was not an "A" student, but probably could have been. I was more focused on validation outside of the home and was in survival mode. I was trying to navigate appearing to have a normal life, while trying to be active, social and athletic.

Every time I ran away, my dad would be at the school the next day to pick me up. We would go out for a snack and a conversation of how I needed to stop running away. He always would let me know how scared and worried I made him when I did this. He would assure me that he loved me greatly and did not know what to do with this situation. In those times, there was no protection from police, social workers, teachers, etc. Even though his life's greatest regret in the end would be not getting us out of the situation, he felt helpless at the time and just tried to manage it.

I was a natural athlete. I used this as a reason to be away from home as much as possible. I participated in Karate, Volleyball, Soccer, Softball and ran Honors track. I thank God today for the opportunity to be involved in these sports and to live close to my high school. I was able to meet and have many friends so that I could endure what was happening at home. I even hung out every chance I could at the handball courts at the school and got pretty good at playing it. The competition, the physical challenges, the discipline and the camaraderie in these sports served me well in tolerating the abuse at home and kept me away from home with acceptable/permitted places to be. When I did get home, I was too tired to give that situation a lot of thought, other than tomorrow was another day.

With dad being the open and loving person he was, he was our rock that kept us somewhat grounded and sane. We knew that one of our parents loved us and was trying to do his best to keep us as safe as possible. He had us 6 kids to take care of along with his parishioners. Being a minister was my father's calling. He took his job as a shepherd of his people seriously. If things got too ugly with mom at the house, we would go next door to the church; we lived in the parsonage (house that belonged to the church). We would just have to knock on the stained-glass window of his office if the church was locked. He would always open the door to us if he was there. He spent a lot of time there, escaping home also. I knew my dad would always be there for me no matter what.

Being a minister's kid, I of course was very involved in the church. Every time the doors were open and many times behind the scenes, we were at the church. I learned some about God, but I wasn't sure about God. I didn't understand why this abuse from my mother was being allowed. I couldn't understand why others did not see what was happening. I was open with my friends about what was going on in my home. I was an outgoing person, caring and accepted my life the way it was, but still had questions. My friends thought I was exaggerating except the few that got to witness the abuse. I brought very few people around my home because I was embarrassed and did not know what my mom would do or say.

Being the beginning of my Senior year in high school, I began thinking what I would do after graduation. I had been working for the past year, putting money away into the bank. My dad was pretty strong about allowing me to spend a portion, but the majority of my paycheck would have to be saved. I was so busy with surviving, being in sports along with also playing my violin in school plays and in the Long Island Symphony. I see now that in my attempt to survive my home situation and due to being a social person, that I kept myself very busy. With the money put away, I believed I wanted to continue my schooling. I was strongly thinking of going to the local community college after I graduated from high school.

While I wanted to attend college, I started worrying about this path. I knew that as soon as I was able, my #1 priority was to get out of my home. I knew that my biggest desire was to escape my abusive mother. I knew that I could not go to the community school, because it would mean staying at home. I had a long-term boyfriend of 3 years by this time, but I was nowhere close to wanting to get married. I didn't have any other opportunities to live somewhere else, so it started to become apparent I had to find another way out.

My dad and I started talking about me possibly going into the military. We went to the recruiting office on Main Street in town many times. I learned of all the opportunities that were open to me. Back then they had the GI Bill that would help me pay for school. There were several choices in duty station available to me upon completion of my training. We were involved in the Vietnam war, but women were not allowed to serve in a war zone, so it didn't frighten me to join. I started to investigate which Military Occupational Specialties (jobs) I would have interest in and what permanent duty station had the strongest appeal to me. I knew one thing for sure; I did not want to be anywhere near my mom.

I love the ocean and warm temperatures, so I wanted to go to California. I wanted to go into Personnel Management MOS because I was interested in working and helping people. As I was investigating all of this, I was told I was not able to join until I had turned 18 years old. At that time, I would need both of my parents' signatures to enlist. I was worried that my mother would not sign the needed paperwork for me to escape her, just out of spite. As my senior year progressed, I stayed busy in my Senior activities along with all the sports and church activities I was involved in. I looked forward to graduation and a new life.

As my time for graduation came, I was excited to have accomplished all my education at that point, but sad to think that I would have to leave friends after high school. My best friend lived in the next town over and her family attended our church. She was heading upstate to college. It felt that the only way out of my home was to join the military. Since I was still just 17, enlistment would have to wait until October 13th, my eighteenth birthday. I graduated towards the end of June, so that meant I had 4 more months of hell before I could leave for the military. That was IF my mom signed the papers. Up until that time, she still had not and was threatening not to. Dad was talking with her to convince her to let me go and explore the world; to let this bird fly free. It took some time and much talking to her until she finally signed my freedom papers. Now the wait until October so I could leave.

In 1973, when I joined the Army, it was still a "Man's Army". There was the Women's Army Corps, so that our basic training and other areas of the military were separate from the men. A major expansion of the WAC began in 1972. The men's draft ended June of 1973. In preparation for this, and in order to maintain the numbers in the military, the Women's Army Corps was expanded. There was a strong recruiting campaign for women along with the opening of all Military Occupational Specialties (MOS) to women at that time except those involving combat duties. The strength of the WAC increased from 12,260 in 1972 to 52,900 in 1978. (online URL: armywomen.org, Women's Army Corps Veterans' Association. 2004-20014).

On October 30, 1973 I was enlisted in the Army at Fort Hamilton, Brooklyn NY. My mother still did not support my decision. Only my dad was there, standing proudly by, watching as I was inducted into the military. I was worried about leaving my dad in that situation since, as mentioned before, he was not exempt from her physical and verbal abuse. I was sad to leave him and my friends, but excited about my future and to be finally free! I went from there to Fort McClellan in Mobile, Alabama. Basic Training would be 6 weeks long, then I would be home a short while for Christmas before leaving again for more training. I was scared and very nervous about what was to come but felt that I could pretty much survive anything due to what I had endured at home. Basic training was hard and challenging. We learned many things along with how to endure being yelled at (knew that already). I was in trouble a lot with my Drill Sergeant, it truly was not intentional, I knew well how to avoid conflict. It seems that because of the way we talked in New York; the inflection of our voice at the end of our sentences, my Drill Sergeant (from Texas) thought I was constantly talking back to her. Now why would I do that?

Due to combat MOSs not being opened to women, we were not trained in weaponry at this time. It was interesting doing Basic with all women, since they had not integrated men and women together for many things yet. Most of my friends in high school were guys because they were less dramatic and emotional. I made a few friends in Basic, but it was mainly to survive it. I had never been out of New York nor met any people outside of my state. It was truly a time of adjustment, but I was FREE. Interesting to me now, looking back that I would go from an abusive home situation into one of mega authority and control such as the military? Maybe I was familiar with the authoritative style, but in fleeing my home/mom, ended up in a similar system.

I knew at the time my main focus was escape and opportunities outside my home town. At times, of course, I had trouble with authority. In the military, you are expected to give respect to those over you or those who outrank you. That was very difficult for me. I felt that people had to earn respect. My mother sure didn't earn it and had abused it, so it was uneasy for me to do that. It was expected to give respect and authority to someone just because they had more time in service or more rank than you.

I grew up in a time when men frequently used certain circumstances to take advantage of women. I learned that at the time I joined the Army, women were still separate in the WAC. They were being assimilated in the "Man's Army". We were beginning to pull out of the Vietnam War when I came in, with it finally ending in 1975. The WAC was disbanded in October 1978, 5 years after I had enlisted. I reenlisted for a second 3-year term, so, I was still on Active Duty during this time. (Women's Army Corps Veterans Association 2004-2014)

As women were assimilated more into what had been mostly a man's military, there were many challenges. Obviously, the men were used to being mostly around men. Basic training became integrated. Basic training had to be modified, as the tasks and challenges were difficult but obviously different between men and women. Young women soon would be side by side with young men in training along with having a man for a drill sergeant. That would bring many challenges and adjustments.

As I finished my all women basic training, I went on to do Advance Training for my MOSs. I did clerical training at Ft Ord in California and Personnel Management training at Ft Benjamin Harrison in Indianapolis, Indiana. I was excited to be traveling, learning new things and meeting new people. One thing that continued to bother me was the problems of integrating women and men into "one Army". I began to see early on that women were objectified and treated poorly. After all we were "just women". It was prevalent thinking at that time that men were more capable serving in the military, and women were not allowed to serve at the front. Eventually in my second 3-year term of active duty, 1976-1979, I was trained on the M-16 rifle. It was very nerve-racking for me, having never been exposed to guns. I was excited to learn, but scared nonetheless.

I know that integrating women into a "men's Army" was not an easy process. I don't know if there was much pre-thought or planning in this process. I can only tell you my opinions and relate to you some of the things that happened to me. Many of these things were kept secret and to myself. In that day and time, if a female would say that she was being sexually harassed or molested, you would become a victim many times over. In addition, you were a part of the military and would worry about someone lying about you and you being dishonorably discharged. There were no avenues for a female to speak out at this time. To this day, it still is difficult as you are aware of all of the stories about sexual harassment throughout the military, especially at the officer schools.

There were incidents of misappropriate statements,

touching under the guise of training, and unacceptable actions. One such circumstance was when I was stationed at Ft Shafter in Oahu, Hawaii. I was newly married to another service member and was reassigned to Hawaii after he came up on an assignment. I was working as a Personnel Management Specialist and clerk to a First Sergeant. The First Sergeant was my boss and there was an officer; a Captain that was his boss.

Fridays were dress down, which is to say, civilian clothes were authorized rather than a uniform. The dress of the day there in Hawaii was halter dresses orshorts with T-shirts. I made my own clothes by then, and would always be appropriately dressed, trying to cover up as much as possible. I was a wife and a military woman, along with having a strict upbringing. I was also blessed with lots of common sense along with thinking through situations ahead of time. This was due to the survival mode I grew up in to make it through my childhood challenges.

Many times, on these Fridays that we were wearing civilian clothes, I was sexually harassed. I was openly ogled, along with inappropriate comments being made. There were times when my First Sergeant would come to my desk to talk to me about something, and openly lean over my desk to try to look down my dress. I was embarrassed and did not know what to do. I would stand up and try to continue my conversation as if it did not happen. At that time, it was not to be discussed with anyone. You knew that there would not be anything done; you were made to believe that because that person outranked you, you would not be believed. I guess we felt rank had its privileges and you had to know your place. My husband had a temper, so I did not discuss this with him.

I felt at the time that it would be better to ignore this behavior as long it did not get too dangerous, and to act like nothing happened. I quickly learned to try to avoid situations that would place me in the line of fire IF at all possible. The feeling that women were sexually objectified was prevalent during my first years in the military. I went from Active Duty to the Reserves after almost 6 years of active duty. I had my first child while on Active Duty in 1977. Becoming a mother was a big deal to me and my strong desire to a better mother than I had been raised by was important to me. I did not have a model shown to me as to what that looked like, but I wanted to give it a good hard try.

I knew I had a lot to overcome, with my abusive past, some hurts and damage that happened while on active duty. I felt that since I had honed my survival skills during my childhood and in my marriage, that in 1979 when I became a single mamma, I would be fine. I knew that I would have to do some counseling and hard work to move on in a healthy way from all that had transpired. It was going to be very hard, but I felt early on in life that I could not control the challenges that were dealt to me as a child. I could control what I did with them as an adult. When you have such a horrendous childhood or anything that has hurt you deeply, you have 2 choices. You either use it as a crutch for the rest of your life, not taking accountability for your actions and always blaming all that is wrong in your life on your past. Your other choice, which I chose in my early 20s, is to do the hard work in counseling and to heal. Along with counseling, I was a Christian and prayed and worked through forgiveness.

I will never regret what happened to me in my childhood, joining the military or any other challenges that have happened since then. These hard things taught me wisdom, perseverance, skills and made me who I am today. I truly believe that when you are born, God knows what you will go through and puts special talents/gifts in you to survive these things. I also strongly believe that we are meant to help others with thisknowledge and the skills we have obtained. We are not to focus on these hurts other than to heal from them. We all have a story, hurts and challenges in our lives. It would be so awesome if we all would do the work to heal from them, forgive and reach out to others going through similar challenges. You cannot have testimonies in your life without the tests.

I am grateful for all that has happened to me, even though at the time these difficult things were   happening, I was NOT. I thank all those who were in my life at these times that helped me. I am very grateful to my dad, that even though he could not get us out of the situation, that he was my rock and stability during that time. He taught me love, perseverance, honesty and openness. He was always talking about loving others in spite of their faults and that we are all flawed in one way or another. He taught me mercy and grace along with forgiveness. We laid my mom to rest a few months ago, and I can say that through forgiveness (which was a lot of work), I was able to be with her more through her last 10 years of life. I moved from Colorado, leaving family, close friends, and a life of 31 years to be by her during the last 8 years after being diagnosed with Alzheimer's until she passed recently. I honored her as my mom regardless of what she did; she was still my mom. I eventually didn't expect her to change or be different. I learned to live and accept her for who she was. I changed myself, got healed and continued to look for ways to be a better me. I will always be grateful for the experiences and opportunities that happened to me and being in the military. I was able to get my education, to meet wonderful people, to travel to many wonderful places and to grow as a person. I will always continue to thank my Dad, my close friends and the Lord for loving me and being with me through it all.

MISS JACK, CAPTAIN
UNITED STATES ARMY

I like to watch how people walk. How people walk, in my opinion, is a good indicator of how they go through life, and ultimately if they live up to their potential. My experience has taught me to watch how people walk to get any indication of how they will be, not only as a person, but also as a leader. I have been wrong at times, and like all things, I've learned to hold judgement. I've learned to watch, observe, and make a decision later on how I can adjust to this person. No, I'm not a stalker or a weirdo who sits around and judges how people walk like it's my job. When you take a second to look around and see what's going on around you, you start to notice things. I like to people watch on a warm sunny afternoon in Florida by the beach, but who doesn't? That's okay sometimes, but daily I watch how people walk and interact with others. I watch how people react to good and/or bad news. Am I a psychologist or a licensed therapist? No, I am a female American Soldier. I have served eight years and I'm currently an Army Captain. I'm not sure if this will be a career, but I can tell you how I ended up here.

What seems like ages ago, really wasn't. I can remember making the decision to join the Army. I was married to an enlisted Infantryman, so I got to 'live it' a little before I made the leap to join the service. I worked as a contractor for the Army, I went to school full-time and held down the home front when my then-husband deployed twice to Iraq. We lived in Alaska, 4,000 miles away from home. At 19, I saw first-hand what the military could do for families, soldiers, and the average "Joe" off the street. While working as a contractor for the military I was able to work directly for and with Soldiers, enabling them to determine their own path to success.

There were two types of soldiers who would walk in the education center building where I worked. The first was a motivated individual, who maybe didn't know how, but wanted to enroll in classes. They were going to make it work in between field missions, personal responsibilities, and his regular job.

The second was an individual who walked in with a deer in the headlights look and they were there to enroll in general education because their sergeant told them to.

I have been fascinated by what makes people tick and what makes them behave the way they do. As a psychology major I grasped the concepts easily. Working for the military as a contractor, and now active duty, I have had the privilege to meet people from all walks of life from across the globe. In my opinion, the sure way to understand a person is to watch how they walk, how they carry themselves. How you carry yourself says a lot about who you are as a person. I am not the final judgement on this earth, but I can tell you how people carry themselves has helped me gain perspective on how and why people do things the way they do, in and out of the military. I mostly relate to people in the military because this has been my lifestyle since I was a young adult.

My experiences in the military, good and bad, have helped to shape me into the person I am today. My experiences to present day haven't all been good; in fact, they have taught me a lesson. I have learned having toxic leaders can give you a definitive picture of exactly what not to do and how their singular actions influence hundreds.

A previous leader had a knack for saying they read the Bible every day, they cared about people and made efforts to have face-to-face meetings with staff Monday morning prior to the work week getting hectic. What this leader did was not walk the walk. This leader would talk over you, interrupt you, ignore your feelings, and cuss out junior officers whom they didn't like. This individual would also 'walk with a purpose' as we say in the military. This meant they didn't waste time and they were always in the mode of getting work done. They were a go-getter and cared very much about their job and the outcome but only if it was their way. They spent the majority of their day in the command sergeant major's office complaining about privates and how the job wasn't getting done.

I say 'toxic' because this leader wasn't effective at leading, but they were effective at demotivating. They had the uncanny ability to make work harder and everything was a top priority. Nothing was ever completed to standard because we were in a rush to get it all done. This person would demand answers for unimportant job-related functions and have you write a book report on citing a regulation reference, send you on a goose chase for a task that wasn't related to your job, then they would apologize to you for unnecessarily yelling at you 2 weeks ago for something perceived to be a slight. To make matters worse, I also saw this person degrade officers in front of their soldiers.

There are many great officers in the Army, we see them every day getting coffee, picking up mail, and picking up cold medicine for sick kids. This officer may walk with his or her head held high, they may walk at a brisk pace or not, and they may carry themselves as an approachable human being. The difference between this officer and a toxic one isn't necessarily how they walk, but how they treat and interact with people.

In the military, when an officer gets promoted early for the next rank, we call them rock stars. These rock stars have this internal switch to turn on their charismatic personality and can seamlessly answer any question, can handle any stressful meeting with ease, and help promote self-identity and assurance in the work place. I misjudged this officer because I used their gait as the measure and after 8 years I've learned it's not *the* indicator, it's not the sole means to judge, it's about their character, integrity, and leadership.

There are many Army values that present in quality leadership. The three above are the most important.

Without your integrity, the perception of you can change in a heartbeat. Great leaders care how they are perceived, they don't act like robots and walk in and out of the front door everyday doing their job. This falls in to character and leadership. The officers who care how they are perceived make an effort to include everyone in the discussion, everyone's ideas matter, they feel a part of the team and valued as a contributor.

I've seen this example to describe a few great CEO's as well. Steve Jobs, Bill and Melinda Gates, Warren Buffett, Ellen DeGeneres, Pablo Isla, Oprah Winfrey, and Michelle Obama to name a few.

I personally believe what sets great leaders apart from their peers is their ability to read a situation and adapt. It's easy to be the boss in a room and point fingers and say 'well I think...' but it's harder to read and understand what makes people tick and how to motivate them. It's easy for me to say adults should always be masters of their behaviors and attitudes. I don't want to degrade anyone's job, but frankly some do not require everyone to be a leader.

A CEO has a wide impact on a company and the business of the day; a front desk security guard of the same building also has a wide impact on the building and day-to-day business, however, the security guard isn't responsible to shareholders or international economic markets, but he has to do the best at his job because the security of a corporate building depends on him.

The Army is built similarly. We have our top leaders who make all of the strategic decisions that have Army wide implications for going to war; we have non-commissioned officers (NCO's) who are responsible for entire convoys getting from base to the field across hundreds of miles. Both have far reaching effects, but on a different level. I highlight the difference not because I believe there is a class system, but because some people have a greater ability to motivate others to live up to their potential. This is more evident the longer I serve. I meet people from all backgrounds and walks of life and some make me question who propped them up to get them where they are. I've had leaders who mentor me and guide me and inspire me to be a better officer and more importantly, a better person.

You know that one person who is awkward, doesn't really fit in and just does what they're told, collects a paycheck and doesn't worry about personal interactions? For every company, formation, unit, or business there is always roughly 10% of the population who has trouble adjusting, fitting in, or adapting due to either personal shortcomings, attitude, or poor mentorship. Unfortunately, in the military, we have more than our fair share of this population.

From a private to senior leadership, they are not equipped to lead soldiers. The Army can be considered one of the largest non-profit fortune 500 companies in the world. Our ability to move people and equipment on short notice is unparalleled. Our ability to get the mission done regardless of resources and time is what sets us apart top corporations, like Apple and Google. We aren't stationary; we are a worldwide deployable force capable of going anywhere at any time when told to for any mission.

What makes a leader in the military is their ability to do more with less. Leadership has no business being on an evaluation. It should be a point of pride.

In 2014, the Disney Institute wrote an article about increasing productivity. It wasn't about doing more with less or who produced the most; it was about listening to your people, getting them engaged and having a voice, and getting their 'buy-in' to the organization.

This translates well to the Army because when soldiers believe in the mission, feel valued, and encouraged, they will voice some incredible opinions and ideas to make things run smoother. The problem here is that 10%, or that awkward soldier as I call them, can hinder possibilities and probably potential. They aren't a natural leader, organization and order are difficult skills for them, and they have a problem motivating, leading, and having meaningful relations with peers and subordinates. They are unrealized potential. They are the group that just misses the mark and just can't get it right. The military can be small, but it can also be big, and when soldiers aren't being mentored, coached, and trained on their job and interpersonal relationships, the organization will suffer.

This type of person has taught me that they can't just turn up the volume, they have one speed setting and it's mediocre. It's okay to be mediocre because this earth needs folks to do jobs the rest of us can't do, the jobs that don't require leadership or much thought- we have regulations, SOP's, and manuals to tell you how to do your job. Where the military got it wrong is they don't invest in talent management from the beginning.

You are a number, able to fill an empty seat with your baggage and all. When the military flexes to grow or reduce in size, so does their quality of people. As a leader, the constant challenge is figuring out how to produce, build a team, establish meaningful relationships, and conduct field training with no accidents or safety issues. When you have a leader who can't bridge the gaps or foster team work, it shows. They are labeled difficult to work with. I have worked with and watched very close friends leave the military because of poorly developed leaders and they just keep getting promoted because we need people who can breathe to fill a role. The Army specifically is giving a voice to the newer generations with the growth of social media to reach more soldiers in a short period of time. They have changed their evaluations system, processes for feedback through surveys and sensing sessions.

While they are on the right track, they still have a long, long way to go.

DIANA FURST, STAFF SERGEANT
UNITED STATES AIR FORCE

I still recall the day Air Force recruiters visited our high school to hand out literature and discuss enlistment requirements. The recruiter's target audience were the young men about to turn eighteen and graduate. With draft registration required, the Vietnam War on-going, and those not given an exemption to attend college or medically deferred, service in one of the military branches would be required for the men. In retrospect it strikes me as odd that an eighteen-year-old male could enlist or be drafted into military service without parental consent, but an eighteen-year-old female needed a parent to sign her enlistment papers. Regardless of the inequity, I was smitten and wanted to join the United States Air Force.

I grew up in an environment where females were expected to marry, stay home and raise their family. So of course, my parents would not even entertain the idea of signing for me to enlist because "nice girls don't go into the military". Remember it was the late 60's!

On the day I turned twenty-one in March 1970 I went to the Air Force recruiter's Office and tried to enlist. But not so fast, women couldn't just enlist, women had to be "chosen" for enlistment by a Selection Board at Randolph AFB, Texas. The first obstacle was the fact I was thirty pounds overweight. But I was determined to join the Air Force. So five months later, after having lost thirty pounds, I sat for the submittal package photographs and took the entrance exams. At the time, AFSCs for women were limited and based on test scores any specialty involving mechanical work was not in my future. But that was okay, a couple of weeks later my recruiter called to tell me "I was in". It was a moment I'll never forget.

In the wee hours of September 10, 1970, I was on my way

to San Antonio, Texas. The final mode of transportation was a bus from the airport to the base, arriving around 3 A.M. We were given breakfast and then shown to the barracks. Now it seemed reasonable that we'd get to sleep in that first morning, but at 6 A.M. a very snarly woman (who we later found out was our Drill Instructor) got us out of our bunks and out the door for another breakfast and to the clothing office for military apparel. Welcome to the United States Air Force!

I'm not going to lie, the first few days were unpleasant. At twenty-one I was the oldest enlistee in the flight and I learned quickly that more was expected of me in terms of leadership and supporting the other women. My standard advice was "it's only six weeks, do not grumble so anyone can hear you and follow instructions". Looking back, a few of the more bizarre things about basic training were: we couldn't speak to a member of the opposite sex, could not use the phone, needed permission to buy a soda, learned to fold a bra into a square, and had room inspections where the DI actually bounced a quarter on the bunk. Lights out meant lights out. Latrine duty was the punishment for getting caught reading a book or writing a letter under a blanket by flashlight.

With our ever present "Ditty Bag", we marched everywhere we went. In the beginning it seemed we marched and pivoted as a form of torture. Weeks later when the flags were added to the marching did it finally connect there was a method to this madness – parade participation. There were classes in military history, protocol, rank structure (if it moves salute it), proper wearing of the uniform, along with hair and makeup application. In those days, we collected our $63.00 pay by reporting to the DI and Finance Officer and saluting was required. I spend a lot of time in front of a mirror practice saluting and will honestly confess to having the worst salute in history of the Air Force.

A few days before graduation from basic, the AFSC and tech school assignments were passed out. As a 906XX, Medical Administration Specialist designee I was headed to Shepard AFB in Wichita Falls, Texas. Tech school was a bit like going to college and a 360 from basic training. After arriving on a Friday evening, we were given the weekend free and could wear civilian clothes in off hours. Our dorm rooms were spacious with an attached bathroom that had a bathtub. The twelve weeks of training went quickly, classes, assignments, and a few KP duties. My KP claim to fame is cutting cherry pies for ten hours and to this day I am not fond of cherry pie.

All 906XX designees were required to participate in a 3-day mass casualty exercise in week four. Bussed to a large pasture in the middle of nowhere we pitched tents, dug holes in the ground for latrines and built fires to keep warm. The menus consisted of C Rations straight from the can and water from a creek that ran through the pasture which had it could go into the canteens. I've always thought this was a weed-out exercise because anyone who fainted at the simulated blood, bones sticking out of wounds or a deceased person was moved into another AFSC. The most memorable experience of the exercise had nothing to do with military learning. On night two, several cows wandered from an adjoining pasture to check out the tents. The cows walked in, the females started screaming, and the cows were so scared they defecated before leaving. It was funny as long as it wasn't your tent with cow manure.

In January 1971, after a short leave back home, I traveled

to my duty assignment at Ehrling Bergquist USAF Hospital, Offutt AFB, Nebraska. There were two big shocks when I got to Omaha. Shock one – disembarking from the aircraft there were literally twenty-foot snow banks from successive winter storms. Shock two – (Husker) Go Big Red toilet tissue. I was sure someone in the Air Force personnel office had a personal vendetta against me. Initially I worked in the Orderly Room under direction of the Squadron First Sergeant. After receiving a promotion to A1C I was moved upstairs to the Hospital Commander's Section. Among the duties in that section, a male A1C and I were the designated escorts for the General Officers and their wives when they came in for care. The Command Area was primarily staffed with Senior NCOs and officer rank medical professionals. It was a busy environment, but I cannot recall a time when I was not treated with respect. My immediate supervisor was a CMSgt who mentored me through the 3, 5 and 7 level advancement and promotion to Sergeant. I was one of the first groups to WAPS test for and be promoted to Staff Sergeant.

At Offutt I wore the Class A uniform to work every day and I have to say I liked it very much. Blue skirts, jackets, lighter blue blouse with a tab tie, beret, black pumps and handbag. During the earliest days of my enlistment earrings were not permitted but that changed a short time later to allow studs. Our utility uniforms were blue twill slacks, blue blouses and low quarter black lacing shoes. Most of our clothing was provided, but we did have to buy our own overcoats, jackets and boots. All enlisted women under the rank of SSgt were required to maintain a room in the dorm and there was more than one snowed-in celebration in the time I lived there. Staying awake all night to pull dorm duty was hard but we all pulled our shifts.

Several significant events that occurred during my enlistment:

- The Vietnam Prisoners of War returned to America in January to April 1973
- The Yom Kippur War in October 1973 when the Ehrling Bergquist World Wide Deployment Team was activated.
- The Air Force awarded military women the same pay and allowance benefits for civilian spouses that male members enjoyed.

A most memorable person from my military days is Ellen. I met Ellen in tech school and, despite the fact we are polar opposites in terms of personality, over forty years later we are still close friends. She is outgoing, and I am more reserved. She was the first to finish college after separation from the military and started a nursing career with the Veteran's Administration System. My degree(s) would come years later but she was there to encourage me when I didn't think I could finish. She was maid of honor in my wedding and I was hers. She is Godmother to my daughter. Had it not been for the Air Force my path would not have crossed with this wonderful lady.

Service made me a stronger person with an exceptional work ethic, team mentality and a philosophy of doing a job right the first time every time. After leaving the military I briefly worked in a university setting before moving into a career with a defense contractor. That career spanned over thirty-six years and the immense pride I feel every time I see the (two platforms I supported) E-3 or E-4B fly over is indescribable. In my mind, being a defense contractor is a privilege and that privilege comes with the responsibility to understand and appreciate military protocol expectations for personal interactions and meetings. That pride is something I strived to instill in younger members of the team who had no previous military exposure.

I separated from the service in April 1974 as part of a first term airman reduction program. I am so proud of having been a member of the United States Air Force and contributing to the defense of a country I love.

DIANA RILEY, SPC
UNITED STATES ARMY

Growing up as a little girl in a small, growing city in Louisiana living in what we call the Hood, I had dreams, aspirations, and visions. I was just an innocent little girl, not knowing the power of dreams and visions. I thought that I could be anybody, do anything; my role models were few and hard to imagine because I didn't see anyone I could model to be like in the hood. I was impressed by and I focused on my school teachers and how they impacted me.

Reflecting back to those times, I understand why I pretended to be a teacher during my play time. My teachers were a strong example of what I wanted for myself. My cousins and I would get together in the back yard near this big tree; the tree is still living but my family no longer lives there. I would be the teacher: the night before, I made lessons and carbon copied every homework sheet to teach my cousins. There was no computer or printer in my house, just encyclopedias--I grew up in the 80's. My cousins sat around in imaginary desks, which meant on the grass sitting Indian style. I had an imaginary classroom: the sunny, beautiful outdoors under a shade tree; it was the perfect environment for our creative, imaginative minds. I kept their attention for a little while until it was time to move on to something else and be adventurous.

I also remember making bows and clothes for my Barbie doll; I'm not quite sure where that inspiration came from. My mama gave me permission to be creative and use my imagination. I helped her garden, cook, and of course I had more than a fair share of chores. Sometimes I would get caught singing in the bathroom or playing in the closet. My bedroom had a huge closet and I would go into it sometimes to hide out and just be me. Maybe I was a misfit for a young black girl growing up in the Hood; maybe not.

My childhood brings back so many memories—certain memories that are good and some memories that are horrible, that I wish I could forget. All in all, it made me who I came to be and molded my adulthood. It prepared me for a future I couldn't possibly have imagined. As I told the story in my first book, *Cooking on Purpose: Life Lessons Learned in the Kitchen*, my education shaped me and caused me to evolve into my purpose. For three years in high school, I participated in Army JROTC, which motivated me to join the military.

By the time I graduated from high school, I was a mother of a 3-month-old baby girl. Going to the Louisiana National Guard was not a quick and easy option for my circumstances. Through trials and challenges, I was able to overcome by God's grace and I enlisted at the age of 23. It was unusual at the time, but I was already in college, married with children, and on the brink of separation with no other stability; I did what was best and what I had always wanted to do after graduation. I became a soldier.

Imagine leaving your children to go serve your country and not knowing what was going to happen. That was me in 2002. Truthfully, I hadn't worried about what was going to happen. My faith was bigger than my fears and I didn't even comprehend what mustard seed faith was at the time. I was fearless. I was relentless. I was determined. The first time I flew on a plane to my basic training is a blurred memory to me but I do remember being a scared, naïve young woman waiting to take my first picture as a soldier. A blank mind and ready attitude with a David-take-on-Goliath courageous personality. Until it came time to be all those things, I was good. Then I was put to the test, throughout basic training, Advanced Individualized Training, Duty Station drilling, and deployment.

In Basic training, I didn't know that I had the strength to endure. The military truly taught me how to overcome the challenges before me, how to embrace the positivity, how to be open to new and fresh beginnings, how to be resilient, and so much more in a short period of time that will last me for a life-long journey. This is great, because I needed to use of all my experiences and lessons sooner than expected.

Its wake-up—zero dark-thirty. I get up and make my bed with attention to details like folding the corners of my bed sheets; I place combat boots dress right dress, put on my PT uniform (no time for shower), march out the door in cadence, then run. One mile, two miles: too easy. In my mind, thoughts are racing, "I got this, you can do this Diana, it will be over soon, keep pushing, run, don't stop." The pain becomes unbearable; my shins are becoming stressed; I see the hill coming up ahead. Oh no! How will I get up and over? Perseverance.

Life is challenging and every now and again the road gets rocky, steep, or hilly; it becomes to exhausting to climb. That is when you develop your character for perseverance. I am grateful for my military experience because my character developed quickly. I had no other choice if I was going to succeed and live up to the courageous personality I had started with. The perseverance is often defined as a purpose or persistence in a course of action, particularly when one encounters obstacles or discouragement.

What I endured before enlisting was challenging enough; I was young and had a certain measure of understanding. I had made poor choices and the only way to cope and overcome was to make better choices. There I stood, having successfully completed Basic Training, and graduated with Honors in Advanced Individual Training (AIT) in my Military Occupational Specialty (MOS); In addition, I had completed a tour of duty in Iraq. What was next? Would I continue to make better choices? Of course, maybe not as poor as I had previously made, but in a different aspect.

I was supposed to do everything I did; however, some of the times, I didn't know what direction or decision to make so I lived on the edge, recklessly doing whatever. Lesson learned: don't do things just because you see someone else doing them. I went to clubs and parties because I had people in my life going out partying almost every weekend, not realizing the effect it would have on my loved ones. When you know better, you do better— and thank God—I got saved and delivered. My military deployment was a factor in my choice of becoming saved. It was a beautiful spring day. I went to church with the intentions of getting baptized at the age of twenty-six. I didn't know that my life was about to change. I was baptized at an old-school traditional church, rich in history and culture. It was my family church, the church I grew up attending, where my mama was in the choir. She wore a choir robe. We wore "church dresses" and my step-dad was a deacon. We would go to church every Easter with our white stockings and Easter hat, and every New Year's Eve, we would be in church kneeling till the strike of New Year's Day but somehow, I missed out on getting baptized as a child. Once again, I have no regrets about this, because I hadn't been mature or educated enough to know what baptism meant. The day I was baptized, I was less than a month away from deployment training.

I knew I needed to get right and dedicate my life to God because I was entering an uncharted territory for me. I would be waking up, counting the days, until I could get some normalcy, whatever that meant. The only normal I knew was the structure set up by the military. Finally, I am home from deployment: "What do I do next?" I don't know. I am struggling to find direction. Who do I want to become; a teacher like I pretended to be, an artist, creator, a homemaker like my mama? Since I am unsure, and I must do something to help take care of my kids, I make a choice. Quick! I go to school to become a pharmacy technician and start working in a pharmacy. Wrong choice. Let me try something else. Nope, that's not working either. I don't know what I don't know.

One of the other better choices I made was to get married to my soul mate, who was also a military veteran. A dual military family, both combat war veterans with a family to raise, was a challenge in its own category. A few years after marriage, I became honorably discharged while my husband was on his second deployment. During this time, I was alone with children to raise and pregnant. My mother had just passed away from cancer months prior to my husband leaving. Here is where my perseverance was put in action. I had no space in my life for a pity party. I was pregnant with my 4th child, we'd just bought a house, my mama had gone to glory and left behind eight children to fend for ourselves, my husband had left for his second deployment, I was in college about to graduate with my first degree, and I didn't know I was dealing with PTSD symptoms all simultaneously. This couldn't be life! This was not my expectations after my previous accomplishments in the military.

I had expected to be married, building a home and rearing my children together with my husband. He would have his career, I'd have mine, and we'd be working on life goals--smooth sailing. Says who? Me, myself, and I. Here's my self-talk: "Okay Cinderella, the clock has struck midnight, you lost your slipper; hurry up and get home back to the reality. Fantasy life is over, for now. Well at least I still have my Prince Charming, right?" Right, married folks, know that Prince Charming is not charming always. Marriage issues arise, parenting issues arise, career issues arise, whatever happened to the better choices I'd been going to make. I did make them, but I came to realize life was not always going to go as I'd planned nor how I'd want it to go. If I could go back in time, I probably would change some of my decisions, but I don't have any regrets about them.

I settled into what my life was at that time and learned to live in the present and embrace the positive. I was open to new and fresh beginnings. It wasn't easy. I admit I had to seek help. I went to therapy and counseling sessions. Giving up was never, ever a choice and it still is not a choice. Although I was married with children and my husband had longevity and stability in his career choice, I didn't. I was a stay-at-home mama trying to feel my way through some things like parenting, loneliness, indecisiveness, and anxiety. I can't give something to somebody that I don't have.

Now, I came to the realization, that faith without works

is dead. The Word is true. I had work to do. I had to be an example for my children, a devoted wife, and be true to myself. It was time to kick the child-like faith back into the game called life. Self-care becomes a needed reality and I started implementing it into my daily routine. Well almost daily. Some days were good, some days were better, yet I persevered. Self-care was not always doing things like getting your hair and nails done; for me it was as simple as lighting some candles, taking a bubble bath while reading a book, with the bathroom door locked. I started a new hobby that soon diminished. I found the time to learn candle making. When my babies were napping, I made candles. Slowly but surely, I was learning to know me better.

As I got my life together to become a better version of me despite the setbacks, challenges and diagnosis, I put one foot forward as though I were marching in formation. Everything I'd done in the military was for a purpose, even if I hadn't understood at the time I was doing it. It was obligatory, but with an intent. One-foot-forward marching resembles looking ahead and not looking back to get to a destination. In cadence--in sync--symbolizes aligning your thoughts with your actions. So, as a man thinks, so he is. I changed my thoughts to positivity through prayer and perseverance. I started to do what was necessary to believe in myself and my dreams. I'd always had a dream of owning a catering company and becoming a published cookbook author. It was time to start thinking out loud.

The hill that was so hard to climb was just a distant memory and constant reminder that I could do it. I could get up the hill and over to the other side. The pain of the difficulty wasn't going to last. As I got over to the other side of the journey, I began to shift my focus and take the necessary steps. It was difficult being a soldier, going to culinary school — pregnant! — with a deployed husband as well as kids at home. That part of my life is over now; it didn't last.

In my spare time (as if I had much, being a mama of five kids), determined as I was, I took online courses, read catering business books, and went to SCORE meetings for small businesses as well as attending business seminars. Slowly but surely, I started my catering business. The process is much too intense to share in one paragraph. Since starting, I lost money and relationships, I must have quit every day and now I have rebranded, and my business is prospering. It is not easy running a business—being an entrepreneur. It takes tenacity, boldness, and the toughness to survive.

Being a military wife, mama, author, and entrepreneur takes perseverance. I had to learn to balance my time. The balance scale never evens out. What makes me effective and successful is prioritizing: I give my attention to what is needed for that specific time. No matter what, I'm always a wife and mama first. My training in culinary arts helps me to keep food on the kitchen table. Sometimes, I'm exhausted like most mamas, so I don't always cook--leftovers get us by. Every now and again we may eat out or order pizza, but that's not healthy. We keep everything in moderation and try our best to eat at home. Of course, you're thinking: She's a chef; that's easy for her to do. I understand the pain of mamas, whether working or not working; we don't always want to cook. My catering company developed a solution and trademark; it's a service for family meals. In the military we ate Meals Ready to Eat (MRE). As a Food

Service Specialist, I cooked in the military; in the field, we had MRE's because sometimes our training schedule didn't allow us to cook. In life circumstances, mamas or daddies can't always cook but we still want a good, nutritious meal for our family.

As stated by Ralph Waldo Emerson, "What lies behind us and what lies ahead of us are tiny matters to what lies within us." This is significant to everything I shared in this chapter. We all can accomplish what we want; we have it in us to so do. The question becomes, are you going to pull out what is on the inside of you--such as perseverance, faith, or courage--to accomplish the goal set before you? There have been times when I lost my mind and was confused, at some points, and sometimes I still get confused, but I have the tools to overcome. When I was in military training, I was assigned a battle buddy. The purpose of a battle buddy was to keep us accountable to each other. In life we must find the accountability we need to stay focused. Yes, life is challenging, life is scary, life is complicated; yet life is good. We have everything we need, and if you can't find it just ask! Someone has what you're looking for. We were not made to do this life alone. Slow and steady is the way. You will get there right when you need to.

I would be unwise not to praise my Savior for getting me through these difficult times, yet I know the perseverance is what He developed in me to endure all that I did. The military helped me to pull this character trait out. It's like the idiom, "If you can't stand the heat, get out of the kitchen," meaning if the situation becomes too much to bear, get out of it. Well, I like to say, if the going gets tough, the tough get going--meaning I set myself to do what I need to do to accomplish the feat before me. You never know how tough you are until you are faced with tough situations. I am a chef, so I'm not getting out of the kitchen. I was not trained to leave a tough situation. Even in my MOS training, I learned in the kitchen. The kitchen is one of the toughest environments you can work in when you're in the "weeds." I have the best of both worlds; I am a professionally trained chef through the military and civilian routes. I was made for this life.

DR. CARLA ANYASO
UNITED STATES AIR FORCE

Paradise Lost

It did not take me long to discover the NCO Club. It was the hottest thing popping on a Friday and Saturday night on base. I was not there long when I met Dion. He was smooth, tall, and had the most brilliant smile that I had ever seen. His body was tight and cut like a Greek God. There was not one ounce of fat anywhere. He had such confidence and his personality filled the entire room. I saw him dancing with another girl, but once our eyes locked everyone else faded away. He asked me to dance and then he whispered into my ear, "Where are you from?" I said, "Chicago." He smiled so bright. He said, "What side?" I said, "I grew up on the North and West Side, but I live on the South Side now." He said, "Hold on. Stay right here. I will be right back." Later, I discovered that he had brought another girl to the NCO club that night, so he rushed and took her home. Maybe finding someone from our home town who understood where we were from, our favorite hangout spots, malls, vernacular, and foods just felt so good. It was like having a familiarity and sense of home in a strange far away land.

From that night on we were inseparable. I don't recall him ever "asking" me to be his girlfriend, it was just understood. I was his, period. And that was just fine with me. Dion had his own car, and an innate leadership, alpha male, and energy that oozed from his inner being. I fell fast in love. I was young, and he was my first real boyfriend since moving from my parent's house. I had never even ridden in a man's car other than my dad's. I was young, free, and trying to soak all of life up in one big gulp. It was all new and exciting.

The day he proposed to me was one of the most beautifully orchestrated days of my life. Every hour on the hour he handed me a single, long, stemmed rose. At sunset, he drove me to a quiet lake on base. As we watched the sun go down, he gave me my 6th and final rose with a beautiful diamond ring. We were married on paper, yet never cohabitated. The day that we were to be wed, every possible omen from heaven came to me to stop it from happening. First, we could not get married in the state of Mississippi because I was not 21 years old. Second, the ATM machine shredded my card, so I could not get the money to pay for the marriage license. Third, we barely made it to the courthouse before it closed to process the marriage license. That night, he dropped me back off at my dorm room and did not return until the next day. He was in no rush to move off base and cohabitate as husband and wife. I later realized that it was because he wanted his freedom to "entertain" other women in his barracks room and continue to exist as a single man.

I also soon discovered, Dion had a diabolical evil streak that seemed to overpower even himself at times. There seemed to be no sense of rhyme or reason that would trigger his erratic, irrational, wild, moody, and abusive behavior. The night time was the worst. He would sleep so wildly. It was almost as if someone were chasing him in his dreams. Almost nightly he would wake up in a panic having a nightmare. Most times he would wake up and say he had a bad dream of his best friend who had died in his arms. He would say that he should have been the one who died instead of his friend.

Through Dion, I learned that all compliments were not compliments at all, they were indiscreet warnings. One day as I looked through a dresser drawer full of pictures from past girlfriends and lovers of his, I noticed a similarity among all the women. They were all fair skinned with long silky hair. On the contrary, I had a dark complexion with a short pixie hair style. I asked Dion why he had fallen in love with me, when every one of his past girlfriends looked so differently. I said, "Based on your past selections of women, you would never think that you would be attracted to me, or even consider giving me a second look." That's when he looked me square in the eyes and said something that sends a chill through the inner core of my soul even now. He said, "You are different because you look just like my mother, and you remind me of her." I smiled and was instantly filled with contentment with his simple explanation. What a compliment because all boys loved and adored their mothers. That's where the terms, "Momma's Boy" originated, right? I learned that was not always the case.

Some people loathed their parents and blamed them for the horrible existence that they called, "life". It was during a visit home to Chicago that I caught a glimpse of the gravity of the emotional pain he was dealing with. A visit to his parent's home provided insight to his "alter ego". Both of his parents were lifelong heroin users. Growing up, Dion was shuffled between foster homes, juvenile detention centers, and his grandparent's homes. He was always in fights or trouble until one day his juvenile counselor suggested that he go to the military. The thought was that a controlled, stable, structured environment would provide direction and the needed change in the familiar surroundings of Chicago. Due to Dion's anger, he carried a deep-seated rage that he would take wherever he went. The military was an element of our external world, but what Dion needed was internal.

Some part of me knew that he was deeply hurting. I thought that he needed me and that all he needed was love. I knew that if I showed him enough love, it would make it better. Yet, at the age of 18, I had no idea of the kind of deep emotional pain and suffering that he struggled with. At that time, I had no idea that pain like that ached. It can't be "loved" away. It can't be given away. It mostly festered, and bubbled out of people like hot lava, spilling out on those around them. Dion and I were off and on. Sometimes he would not talk to me for days. I would pace the floor and barely sleep trying to wait up for him. Each day I would make countless trips back and forth to his barracks room in search of his whereabouts. I attempted to make sense of this mess of a dysfunctional marriage. Yet, I knew immediately that I had made a terrible mistake, and I wanted out.

I can recall the day that my world turned upside down and my internal and external utopia was destroyed. I was sick. I had gone to "Sick Call" and the doctor diagnosed me with a severe urinary tract infection. I had never experienced pain like that before. My kidneys were on fire and caused excruciating pain in my mid to lower back. I felt nausea, lack of appetite, and was physically weak. I can recall that I could barely walk or stand upright. I was also dehydrated. Then Dion came over to visit in my dorm room. I began to explain how sick I was, but he had no real empathy for me. He asked if he could he stay. I was too weak to resist or argue so I relented. He wanted to lay down with me. My sides were so sore, that I preferred pillows propped up, but again, Dion was relentless.

Finally, his real motives surfaced. He wanted to have sex. In the condition that I was in, there was no way that anything of that nature was possible. I told him no and asked him to leave. That is when my naïve, kind, unspoken gentleness left my body and soul. He held my arms above my head with one hand, and pried my legs open with his legs and other hand. I cried and screamed for mercy. The pain that I felt was excruciating. I don't know which cried louder or longer, my feeble voice or my broken soul. But I cried, and cried, and cried. When I finally woke up, I looked over at him and I instantly knew that I was infected. I now was a carrier of what he had been clothed with for an entire lifetime: rage, guilt, pain, hurt, and a broken spirit. I wanted to slit his throat. He jumped up and acted as if nothing had ever happened and that he had done nothing wrong. Yet, he did. I told him "NO." I did not want to have sex with him. He was wrong. I hated him and everything about him.

I suffered many more physical attacks on and off base from Dion. One time, he slapped me so hard in a parking lot that he knocked the sun glasses off of my face and they were shattered. Another time, he grabbed me by the neck and slammed my head against the cement block barracks wall so hard, all that I could do was lift my hand to the back of my head and check to feel the warm blood that was oozing out as a drip or a pour. I was convinced that my head was cracked in two. The sound echoed so loudly that the three airmen living on the second floor raced up to see what the commotion was. When they discovered that I was being beaten, they pulled him away and I ran for my life. I didn't have on shoes or anything. A friend took me to her off-base housing where I stayed for days in fear. I was too afraid to return to base for clothes or anything.

At the urging of friends, I went to the base police station to file a report, but I was told that there was nothing that could be done without witness reports. It was my word against his. However, they acknowledged my swollen lip and face. Our First Sergeant called me into his office one day and asked what I wanted him to do. He said, "Am I to ruin this airman's career over a domestic dispute?" I told him, "I just wanted to feel safe." To my detriment, safety was not to come for me.

Dion was a master manipulator, and I was now public enemy #1. It never occurred to me how a person survived with two parents as heroin addicts from birth and what lessons that they learned from them along the way. If I were a defenseless doe, then he was a trained archer who was hungry with sights on his prey. Dion then began his targeted psychological attack aimed at destroying my credibility and professional standing.

He wrote letters to my First Sergeant stating that I was a known whore on base. He trusted me, and he only acted violently against me based upon the hurt that he felt because of my indiscretions. He then stole several checks from the back of my check book and purchased large ticket items. This caused my bank account to become overdrawn through vendors on base. This was reported back to my leadership on base. I was made to go to psychological counseling and ordered to stay away from him. Basically, I was now a "trouble-maker". I did not fit the model of an Air Force Airman. I brought undue negative attention to myself and my leadership, and in the military my job was to report to duty and go home and stay out of trouble. My sergeant once asked me was I a "party girl"? He then handed me a wet wash cloth and told me to go into the bathroom to clean myself off. He found that I smelled of too much perfume and my lipstick was too "loud". I just went in the bathroom and obeyed. I had worn two drops of vanilla perfume oil from Bath and Body. I knew then that without a doubt, Dion was a dark cloud of trouble that I could not hide from or escape. His attack was personal, diabolical, and locked in on its target. My sergeant's comments to me also proved that his attack was effective. I felt as though everyone who was supposed to be there as my support system and military family were against me. I was far from home with no real family and everyday seemed to be a long nightmare.

As a medical technician in the hospital on base, the only glimpse of solace that I found was there with my patients. The long 12-hour shifts, 7am-7pm, would have been grueling to someone else, but my veterans needed me. The long hours allowed me to focus only on my work. I worked on a cardio-thoracic care ward. This ward was an ICU step-down unit which provided care for patients immediately before and following open-heart surgery. We only held the patients for a maximum of 5 days of post-operative care. Therefore, the unit was a fast-paced, high-volume, high-turnover rate hospital ward. The hours melted away quickly as we all worked hard with over 30 or more patient rooms under my care each day. That was just the diversion I needed to my after-work life. I felt a sense of pride and accomplishment after all my patients were bathed, bed linens changed, fed, vital signs taken, and food trays taken away. They were so appreciative of the care that I provided. I loved my job. Working with the veterans and providing direct patient care was my peace.

As far as my life with Dion, my day of vindication was soon to come. I had no idea, although I learned that sometimes vindication is not always the best thing to hope for. Vindication is a form of validation needed for healing. I would later learn that true validation does not come from the respect of others. In order to accomplish true healing, self-validation, freedom, and peace it must originate from within. Only when I no longer needed people to understand that I was right, I was no longer the victim.

Due to many more complaints, assaults, and altercations, Dion was eventually given the option to separate from the military. He was banned from entering the base. The SP's (Security Police) assured me that his picture was posted with others who were banned at every entry point on base. I was again safe, and his reign of terror was over. During that time, I had just gotten a landline telephone put in my dorm room with a separate caller ID box. It was a new technology that had just come out and there was a free trial. I liked the ability to see who was calling and have the option to answer the phone or not. Dion was still calling and sending letters to my base address. I would not allow myself to read the letters or even listen to his messages. At that time, I had found a church right outside of the gates of the base; and since I did not have a car, it was a perfect haven for me to go and find tranquility.

Soon, things were finally getting back to normal. Many of my fellow airmen who had arrived when I had received orders, made rank, gotten married, or pregnant, all of which made them candidates to move on or move off of base. So, the climate was changing and new batches of younger airmen fresh from Basic where moving into the dorms. I was glad because none of them knew of the drama that I experienced, and it was a clean slate with new friends.

I even had a new suite mate who was nice, and we got along well. In the barracks, your rooms and roommates were assigned to you. At that time since I was more senior enlisted now, I had a room to myself. However, my suite mate was the dorm room on the opposite side of your room or next door to your room in which a shared bathroom connected the two rooms. My suite mate always had a habit of either leaving the door to her side of the bathroom open or leaving her window open. She was a bit of a free spirit.

That day I laid in bed, the phone rang. It was Dion. I forgot to check the caller ID. I spoke to him and he said that he was getting acclimated to Chicago. He missed me and loved me. He sounded so sweet on the phone and convincing. I almost believed him. He had such a way of reeling me back in and making me feel as if I was the only girl on earth and in his world, yet the sexually transmitted disease that he left me with proved otherwise. The day that he raped me, I am convinced that he knew that he had already contracted it. Yet, he wanted to utterly ruin me from the inside out. Seeking treatment among my friends, doctors, nurses, and fellow airmen at the medical center where we worked was the most humiliating experience of my life. Word spread throughout the hospital, the base, and the barracks like wildfire. A little was added and the story and allegations grew.

During my follow-up visit the doctor said that it was treatable and that I would be fine with time. However, my uterus looked "odd", and my pap smear had come back as "irregular" although the STD was cleared. I had to come back for further testing. The results finally came back after a week, and the irregular cells were not cancerous or any other abnormality. I was too afraid at the time to further probe the doctor to expound on why he thought my uterus appeared odd. However, to this day I am convinced that the reason that I have had infertility issues originates with Dion and the irreparable trauma that he caused to my reproductive organs and body. In my entire life, I have only experienced one pregnancy which brought about the birth of my miracle baby girl Bianca. People tell me that I should feel grateful for the ability to at least have her. And I am, yet as I tried for many years to conceive and even now, my mind can sometimes slip and drift away before I can catch it to that dark faraway place. The mystical yet tormenting land of *What if?* What if, I had never gone to the NCO Club that first night on base? What if I had never met the monster? What if. What if. Would I have a son or another daughter? What if. What if.

However, on that day, I just lie there. It was a dark day. I tried to calm myself back into a lull of sleep when the call was over. Only God would not let me sleep. Instead, I decided to glance over at my caller ID box. Instantly, I was paralyzed with fear. I was about to die, and today was going to be the day. My God, My God, My God was the prayer that ran through my head. 'Lord, please help me,' was the prayer that I was too afraid to whisper. Yet, I knew I did not want to die. I could not allow it to happen, not like this. Not now. My mother, I was her first born. My grandmother. All of the people raced through my head. I was afraid to move, afraid to make a sound and afraid to run.

Dion was steps away from me. He lied. The caller ID revealed the truth that he was right next door calling me only seconds ago from my suitemates phone. My mind was blank, and I could not remember whether I had locked my side of our adjoining "Jack & Jill" bathroom door or not. If I had, I was safe for a while. If I had not, he could enter my room at any given second. I was afraid to leave, or he would chase after me and overtake me. If I tried to check whether the bathroom door was locked, he may be just on the other side by now and bust in at the sound of any rustling. His primary objective was to 1. Ensure that I was home alone in my room. 2. Catch me by surprise. 3. Cause me grave harm because he believed that I was the reason that he was no longer in the military. He wanted revenge, and he drove all the way back from Chicago, was able to sneak on the back of the base shuttle bus and was in waiting hiding like a hunter before he strikes his prey.

After what seemed like an eternity, I decided to use my newly installed phone to call 911. I whispered to the police officer that I was afraid. I gave him my building and room number and told him to please come as soon as possible that someone was in my suitemate's room hiding to kill me. Soon the police arrived. Two came in my room and two went in my suitemate's room to search. Two guarded the doors. I heard screaming and four officers drug Dion out of my suitemate's room with a sharpened knife in his hand. He was hiding in her wall locker. As they pulled him out in handcuffs all I can remember is him staring me dead in my eyes screaming, "I hate you!!! I HATE YOU!!! I'm going to kill you bitch!!! I'LL BE BACK. I fell into the officer's arms and cried until I passed out. All I can remember are the words the older Caucasian SP told me as he held me and looked into my eyes. He said, "You are one lucky girl. You are very fortunate to be alive." I can't even recall the rest. My mind has blocked out some details to protect me I think, and others I recall so vividly to protect me also. Some information was forgotten to protect me so that recovery can be attained and some to remember so that it never happens again. It's kind and cruel how the human mind works. Later that week, two of my sergeants were informed of what occurred and I was ordered to move to an undisclosed location on the base. My sergeants moved all of my belongings. The breach in security was not easily corrected. Some shuttle bus drivers that transported military and veterans to the mall and certain sites off base were diligent to check the military ID of each and every person who entered the bus, and some were not. Therefore, I could not be 100% sure that Dion could not sneak back on base again.

My Maslow's Hierarchy which was full only a couple of years ago was now empty. I did not feel safe, I had no friends that knew 100% of all that I had endured and being on the base was just a reminder of each day of my paradise lost. Soon, I sunk into what I now know is a very deep depression. It showed up in my work. I then learned and mastered the art of behavior. I could put on a smile and perform and be fully functional at work, yet when I got home on my off days, I was in pajamas and bedridden. At home I was emotionally bankrupt and never left the house until it was time for work again. It was a struggle to even wash my own ass. So, I didn't. This is a pattern of behavior that I battled for over a decade when depression and the dark days hit.

Soon after being almost murdered in my dorm room, I was told that I was not a good fit for the military. It was decided that I would get a "General, Under Honorable Conditions" discharge. I was angry that I was not granted a fully Honorable discharge, but I was told that anything was better than dishonorable. I had to begin out processing off base. Many friends and co-workers told me I could stretch the out processing for over a month so that I could earn a few more checks, and buy myself some time to get an apartment, other personal belongings, etc. However, I was tired. I wanted out more than anything. I wanted to be done with the military, the memories at my first and only permanent duty station, and anything associated with it. I got an apartment off base, furniture, and out processed in less than a day. My sergeant was amazed. He said that he had never in 20 years saw someone to out process as fast as I did. He seemed concerned and asked what my plans were. He wondered if I would go back home. I was thinking, *Are you crazy?* My mother told me to stay in until I retired after 20 years. I'd still only be 37 years old. I'd be set for life. I would not tell my family right away. I'd wait another year or so until my enlistment was up for renewal and just tell them I decided not to re-enlist. After I cashed out my unused leave, I had enough money to pay up my rent for months and I was free. I asked my aunt if I could get my phone number under her name as well as other traceable utilities. She agreed. I did not want anyone to find me, especially Dion.

I closed this chapter. I was done, and it was never to be spoken of or reopened for many, many years. Only then I didn't open it back up, it came out all on its own, and when it did it was scary. From the moment that I was raped, I did not realize that I was scarred with invisible wounds. I did not know that I had been unwillingly strapped in to a roller coaster ride called, "Post

Traumatic Stress Disorder (PTSD)" caused by "Military Sexual Trauma (MST)". I had no idea that not receiving treatment, counseling, or support from the military for the trauma that I suffered while on active duty would send a ripple effect in so many other areas of my life. If I could only have written a letter to the teenage girl that I was then, I would've told her to hold on. I would've told her to be strong. I would've told her that help was on the way.

JASMINE BOGARD, CAPTAIN
UNITED STATES AIR FORCE

I often say if Texas should (finally) secede and take all its US military members with her, we would be a force with which to reckon! Perhaps we would be the third or fourth world power in terms of military might! Yes, I am a Texan. I often struggle with how to describe myself. If I list the attributes of who (I think) I am, is that socially understood to be a ranking order of precedence? Should I omit the obvious? Is it advisable for me to expound upon what those single adjectives or nouns mean to me? I began with Texan because it was light-hearted, and *everyone* knows "how we are." So, in no order of attributed value: I am a woman. I am Black. I am a daughter. I am a sister. I am an Airman. I am a friend. I am a former legalistic Evangelical Christian. I am a student. I am a free spirit with a gypsy soul.

I firmly believe that experience is the best teacher one can have in life. Our predecessors are runners-up. (Why live through an avoidable "suck" if someone's history has already forewarned us?) Each phase of, and occurrence in, my life has brought me to this moment, to this place, to this mindset. While that may seem an obvious consequence, I am consciously attributing my present state and state of mind to my choices and to decisions of others, whether they were made directly for/to me, or indirectly and from which I was impacted. Experience, family, friends, mentors, co-workers, acquaintances, and frenemies blew mild or strong gusts of wind that affected my life course. Each of them along with my attributes are interconnected. Because of my family I am an Air Force officer. My siblings are why I am a Longhorn. The military is why I can feed my addiction for formal education and travel.

At times my attributes cannot peacefully co-exist

simultaneously. For example, some days I am treated starkly different around central Oklahoma when in uniform than I am in civilian attire, or "civvies." I do often charge that Oklahoma City is a large metropolitan with a small-town mindset. This accusation is apparent with negative and awkward encounters I have had around the city. However, while in uniform I am often treated like a hero and seen. (By "seen" I mean more individuals make eye contact with me and provide a non-verbal greeting, or do not give a nonverbal slight which I have received in civvies.) During the climax of the #MeToo movement and the seemingly constant stream of news covering black men (and women) being murdered throughout the nation, there exists an inner struggle. The dichotomy between me being a black woman who has not personally faced overt sexism or racism in my career field and interacting with military members and civilians who have, is not a fact I take for granted nor ignore. I am not seeking discrimination; rather, I strive to use my position and lessons learned to be that proverbial voice for the voiceless, a reliable mentor, a resource and a pillar of hope and positivity. Informally, it is my role to educate those who are shielded from such realities and may not understand the experience of a black, a female nor a black female in America. I have a confession. I hesitated in writing *too much* about race and sex because I know eyes roll and eyes close at these topics. I quickly slapped my own hand, though, because if I do not initiate and solicit such conversations (which are what is missing in our country-conversation!) how can understanding, progression and true healing occur? Thus, if you have verbally or inwardly sighed in distaste for the topics or muttered, "This again?!," please take some time to reflect on why you reacted the way you did. What would it cost if you empathetically placed yourself in a non-white, non-heterosexual's shoes and learned about their world? Are you willing to trade places for a year? If not, why not? (Maybe those reasons are why "the struggle" still exists.) Thank you for derailing with me for a bit and thank you for listening.

Oddly, I come from a military family, but I am not a military brat. My mom, dad and stepdad each served 1-2 terms in the Air Force. I had an uncle in each branch and family members who served in WWII, the Korean War and in several Middle Eastern countries. I did not have much exposure to the military nor that way of life, but each time the topic arose around my family it was mostly a positive message. I do not know when I decided to pursue joining the military as a serious career option. Admittedly, I thought the Air Force was full of weak pansies; thus, I determined to enlist in the Army or Marines after earning my bachelor's degree. My uncle and mother convinced me otherwise. In fact, my uncle strongly encouraged me join a university's Air Force Reserve Officers' Training Corps (ROTC) while I pursued my degree then commission as a lieutenant. I heeded his advice. After researching schools and programs as well as visiting various campuses across the nation, I realized that if I join the military I will be forced away from family for long periods of time. Family being the most important factor in my life, I was saddened and decided to pursue a local school. Since I did not have funds saved for college and would have to pay whatever tuition and fees my earned scholarships did not cover, I figured it would make the most sense for me to attend a junior college to accomplish my prerequisites then transfer to a university. Additionally, I accomplished dual-credit courses in high school, so it would be a seamless transition to attend full time. Locale- check, type of school- check. I was progressing in my decision tree. I had no idea what I wanted to study, though. I began with my passions. I had been a substitute teacher for a while and loved being in the classroom. I earned an Associate of Arts in Teaching.

For decades I have been interested in different cultures and all their associated sociological and geopolitical phenomena. As an Austinite, I had exposure to Mexican culture, had "studied" Spanish in high school and had *token* friends from whom I could direct my inquiries of "all things" Mexican. (Studied is in quotations because my foreign language classes were like most in US education- a joke. All research verifies that the best time to learn a language is as an adolescent. This perpetual delay of language training places our children behind international peers and reinforces the ethnocentric, English-is-all-you-need mindset!) In 2006 while on a mission trip in Europe, I had limited contact with an Iranian, whom I ignorantly called an Arab (#'Merica) and became enthralled with Middle Eastern culture. It was then I determined to learn all I can about Middle Easterners and study Arabic. Thankfully, the University of Texas at Austin (hook 'em!) had a renowned Arabic/Middle Eastern Studies program. I confess, I did not consider attending UT because that was the popular choice and where mostly everyone wanted to attend, and I make it a point to not follow the crowd. At my uncle and mother's prodding, I visited the ROTC detachment's recruiter. When I told the recruiter I aimed to study Arabic his eyebrows went up and he said the military will fund my education if I qualify for a scholarship. It took me about 1.5 seconds to affirm my interest in the detachment and the school's program. I then met the detachment commander and after hearing my intentions his brow furrowed. He stated UT is quite difficult to get into and recommended I look into an HBCU (Historically black college and university) since their barrier of entry is much lower and since I would have free tuition as a cadet. Taken aback, I reaffirmed then solidified my decision to transfer to UT. It was the only university to which I applied once I finished at the junior college.

I still have not learned my lesson, but sometime during my Junior semester I took on way too many commitments. Not only was I in my third year of Arabic, I had a leadership position in ROTC, was active in my church, enrolled in Persian/Farsi language courses and I decided to pledge a sorority. I really do not know what I was smoking. Alas, my grades suffered, and I did make a high enough grade to progress in Arabic as a major. I could not retake Arabic III since I was on a timeline for ROTC. Thankfully, my military scholarship was a merit-based one and not allotted to me for my degree choice. I was able to major in Middle Eastern Studies (MES) and minor in Arabic and still have my school funded. I would like to say I learned a valuable lesson, but as I mentioned when I introduced this paragraph, the struggle is perpetually real. In introspecting, I think I have this fear of missing out. There are so many things for which I have a passion and would like to learn and experience. As long as I am able to appropriately prioritize and balance priorities, why can't I pursue my interests? I still have not found that sweet spot. I do, however, aim to do all things with excellence and learn from each involvement and encounter. There is so much to do and so little time! If I may divert for a bit- another struggle I have is living in the moment. Because my life's bucket list is so long, I have found myself anxiously seeking how to cross off the subsequent item in the midst of participating in another.

Crazy. I am now more conscious about being mindful in the moment and ensuring I do not live life behind the screen of my camera, phone nor checklist. To my credit, when reminiscing, I actually do periodically look through the hundreds of pictures I snapped.

The next big decision I had to make in college was for which career in the Air Force I intended to apply. As I stated, I am not a crowd-follower, so pilot was definitely out of the running. I also despised the thought of sitting at a desk all day, every day. (Ha! Joke is on me...) I consulted father Google and chose Air Battle Manager (ABM). To my joy, Uncle Sam granted my desire. At the time of my search, and still to this day, there is not much information that explains in layman's terms what an ABM's job is nor what his/her day-to-day looks like. I was relieved that while in training a peer asked if we should expect to fly every day, and if not, what the heck would we be doing? Mostly deskwork. Six years later it has not killed me, though. After the ROTC detachment announced our career assignments, those of us allotted to operations could wear flight suits. I was excited about that! As far as I can recall, I was the only one within a couple of years in my age range who applied for or received and ABM assignment out of ROTC. When I look back at my ROTC years they are mostly positive feelings. I do wish, however, that I would have been more involved with some of my fellow cadets. Because I lived over 25 minutes away with no traffic, and was spread thin with other commitments, I did not spend as much time at the university nor with my peers as I now deem I should have.

Studying MES in AFROTC at UT afforded me the privilege of being involved in various culture and language endeavors for cadets. Dedicated employees such as Christina and Kimberly had the thankless tasks of developing vignettes and planning events for the school and military's partnership pilot programs while wrangling us students and ensuring there was value added to our experiences. Cadets from each service were invited to attend periodic lectures at our detachment. While snacking on a dish from the presenter's country of origin, we learned about stereotypes, geopolitical history, international relations, and current areas of concern. I was blessed to travel to both Morocco and Egypt to study both Modern Standard Arabic and the countries' local dialects. I gained lifelong friends, acquaintances and invaluable lessons.

In 2011, many newly commissioned officers had to wait several months before moving to their first base. Some were compelled to seek employment to pay for living expenses and student and military loans. Fortunately, I was packed and on the road in less than four months. I am quite an independent individual and for several years had been a worldwide traveler, sometimes by myself, but the prospect of a new adventure seemed ominous and somewhat overwhelming. Each previous time I left on an odyssey, I always had a two-way ticket, a home and family unit to which I knew I would soon return. Obviously, this was more permanent. (Hence the name's process, Permanent Change of Station.) The first time I was conscious of my subliminal feelings was at a going-away celebration my church's youth leader hosted. Josh and his wife graciously opened their home to several families. I was surrounded by church and blood family and during the more formal portion of the evening my best friend Amanda and I had a heart connection of sorts and to my surprise, the tears streamed. Although I was overcome with shock and sadness at the open-endedness of my future, admittedly I was a bit embarrassed at my temporary loss of self-control. Good thing those folks love and tolerate me.

At that time my family and I had three large dogs. One was a rabble-rouser and continuously bullied another. One day the scuffle escalated to a full-blown fight between the two with the third attacking the stronger of the two when she had the weaker one (the bully, go figure) pinned down at the neck. As luck would have it, I was home alone and started to panic. I called animal control on myself and the three girls (insert eye roll) and followed the truck to the veterinarian to have both the culprit and victim checked. Knowing the victim, who was both bigger and stronger than the mean girl, would continuously allowed herself to be picked on, I was compelled to keep her and have her move with me. (When we first rescued Lucy, she showed signs of abuse as she would cower and submit to dogs of comparable size or larger and duck her head whenever voices were raised around her. For several months Lucy received Sable's attacks without retaliating.) Initially I was concerned that I would not be able to handle her and my new life, but I was determined to make it work. Essentially, I viewed myself as a single mother who will do what is necessary to care for and protect her baby. Another pleasant surprise of my journey was the addition of my father. My dad agreed to accompany Lucy and me to Florida to help me drive, care for Lucy and get settled.

We had an exciting and memorable road trip. I am thankful I was able to experience some of those *firsts* with him- first relocation, first base, and first time stopping at some of the sights we did. I am not convinced that he would not trade his lungs for gills if given the choice, so to awe-inspiringly behold the vastness of the ocean by his side was a privilege and joy. We stayed in the Temporary Lodging Facility (TLF) for a long while before moving into a more permanent homestead. He loved being so close to the water and having ample opportunity to fish. He rented an apartment in Panama City and I lived on base. I have made a concerted effort to have zero regrets in my life, solely lessons learned. If I did have any though, one that would top the list is the unfortunate fact that I did not cherish our time living together. I was more concerned with 'embarking' and being on my own than with cultivating and strengthening our relationship. Each time I beg him to come live with me, a small voice sends an accusatory reminder that I also asked for space. I did not have a complete appreciation of how much he supported and assisted me until I moved to Oklahoma by myself (as a single parent.) Moving a household's worth of items, and a cat and dog while coordinating storage and house-hunting in addition to processing into the base and the new unit is a daunting, taxing and stressful task. Ah yes, over the span of my young adult life until now, I have had this odd tendency of acquiring four-legged furries. The newest addition to our family was a mean-spirited tom cat who expressed all emotion through his teeth and claws.

The TLF at Tinker Air Force Base (AFB) in Oklahoma City seemed more like a punishment than hospitality. I wanted to uphold its purpose and ensure our stay was indeed temporary. Regardless, I had only a handful of days to locate housing before the military would no longer fund temporary lodging. I was at my wit's end with searching, every avenue I tried failed.

Serendipitously, the final night of my government-funded stay found me desperate and searching one final time through Craigslist housing posts. I responded to what seemed to be a legitimate person and scheduled an appointment to view the property (and introduce our pets) the next day. With a packed car, an anxious pup, and a grumpy kitten, I drove out of the city and entered the five acres located off the unpaved road. It was a roomie match at our first "hello!" Chris was so welcoming and friendly and he and his precious dogs, Mojo and Cotton, fell in love with Lucy. I liked living there, but I was not a fan of being so far from the city center, especially since I was getting more involved in urban activities.

I was thankful to finally graduate from training. Unfortunately, my transition to an operational squadron where I would be flying and controlling solo occurred simultaneously with the first round of sequestration in 2013. Our Wing persevered and I eventually was able to become a functional part of the operations team. I could not tangibly identify the issue then, but my peers and elders now regularly discuss the lack of mentorship in our career field. Although the climate has improved since I initially entered training, we have been known to "eat our own." Thankfully, I have encountered several individuals who have pulled me aside to offer me guidance and when asked, have agreed to provide their perspective and advice. Additionally, I am excited that I have intelligent, dependable peers with whom I can collaborate and from whom I can ask for assistance, guidance and course correction. I welcome the challenge to be the change I want to see and with my peers, implement the values and lessons of servant-leadership, empowerment, career development and mentorship.

I have learned so much from my time in and around the military. Sadly, time and space do not permit me to expound upon the exceptional leader I had as a ROTC cadet in my second detachment commander, Col (Ret.) Bowman. I neither realized nor fully appreciated the benefit of many of his decisions. He (and his bride) are effective leaders who genuinely care with whom I am in contact to this day. I also could not share additional hurdles such as my medical experience which threatened my expulsion from the military and paused my career progression. Although I have experienced challenges and have periodically questioned my place and purpose in the armed forces, the personal, mental, relational, spiritual, professional and emotional development that has occurred is owed to my time in the military and all the influencers prior to me joining who played a part in grooming me for this way of life. To my family, friends, mentors and peers, thank you!

KATHERINE "JOYCE" POFFINBARGER DURHAM STOTLER, SGT UNITED STATES NAVY

"This Happened"
By Katherine "Joyce" Poffinbarger Durham Stotler
US Navy WAVES AK3 1959 – 1961
OKANG TSGT 1975 – 1997
Ready Reserve 1997 -1998

In 1950, when I was ten years old and living outside Astoria, OR in Navy Heights with my Mom and Step Dad (my father having died when I was eight of TB and Diabetes) On a Saturday, myself and about a dozen other Navy brats were at the main gate of the Tongue Point Navy Station awaiting the bus to take us home from the Saturday afternoon movie. Across the road was a BOQ (Bachelor Officer Quarters) and this lady in uniform came out. One of the boys asked the Shore Patrol on guard duty at the gate, "WHAT'S SHE?" The SP said, "She's a WAVES". The boy asked, "What's a WAVES?" and the guard said, "She's a lady sailor". I thought to myself, that is what I will be when I grow up. When I got home I told Mom and Dad "I am going to be a WAVES when I grow up! They said ok, never thinking I would even remember that, but I did remember.

Now fast forward to 1958. I had graduated from high school in Greensburg, IN, where my Dad was the U.S. Navy recruiter for a three-county area. Mom had only a 10th grade education and had worked as a waitress or bar maid all her life. She wanted me to go to business college so I could have a sit-down job.

I attended Indiana Business College for seven months in Indianapolis. I lived in a local business family's home and took care of their three children in the evenings in exchange for my room and board. I was allowed one weekend a month, and one week at Christmas, off. They were very kind and included $5.00 a week in pay. This was all arranged by the Business College.

I did ok in college until they started teaching shorthand. To understand shorthand, you already needed to know phonics, and most people got that at a young age. I was taught a flash card system, and when the rest of the shorthand class was on the page 120 I was still on page 24. I decided business college wasn't for me, after all.

When I went home at Christmas, I told my folks that I now wanted to join the Navy. I took my initial test for the U. S. Navy in my bedroom on that Christmas afternoon in 1958.

While I waited to get a slot, I had my Step-Dad's last name legally added to the end of my name. I had only used Durham since I was 8 years old. Mom figured it wasn't anyone's business how many times she been married, so kept my birth father's last name. I was glad I did because years later, I found out It was a 10th generation American name.

Even though my dad was the recruiter, there was a waiting list for the 5,000 women allowed at any one time in the USN WAVES. Thus, it wasn't until March of 1959 when I arrived by train at the US Naval Training Center Bainbridge, Maryland for my Boot Camp.

About a third of the way though the ten weeks of Boot Camp, the Drill Instructor was not having a lot of luck with getting Company 7 to march in step. She stopped us and said, "Is there anyone here that does not like to march?". I raised my hand. Grandma always said, "Don't lie!" She told me to meet her that afternoon after classes. To the surprise of my Drill Instructor and myself, about a half dozen of the other members of the company showed up as well. When asked why they were there, one of them told her it had been discussed, and they felt everyone should come because Durham was the only one who had been honest. Among our group, nobody enjoyed marching, so they felt it was unfair for me to show up for extra instruction alone.

We marched for a while until the Drill Instructor stopped and said, "Durham, you do not march all that bad." I answered, "Chief, you did not ask if I could march- you asked if anyone did not like to march!" She dismissed us and the next day I was named Right Guide of the Company; the person everyone in the Company guides on when marching as a large group.

In Company 7 most of us went by nicknames. My bunk from South Bend, IN, who was called 'Cowboy', assigned most of our names. Since my last name was Durham, and I had often been called "Bull" in High School, Cowboy changed it to 'Bullface'. Cowboy named her best friend 'Frankenstein'. One of the gal's names was Johnny and she had been a semi-pro basketball player.

When we made our visit to the psychiatrist he asked me, "What did your father think of you joining the service?" I said, "I guess he did not care; he was my recruiter." Then he asked, "Well what did your mother think?" I told him, "My dad is really my step-dad, so my mother had to sign for me. Since she signed, I guess she was ok with it."

There was one other gal who was recruited by her boyfriend; she was the oldest there at 23. The two of us never had to make a second visit to the psychiatrist. Johnny had to make the most visits. She came in after several visits swearing that the psychiatrist was crazy! "He thinks I should hate my parents because they gave me a boy's name! That is my Granddad's name and I very proud of that!"

The other gals all wanted to know why the 23-year-old and I had only had to go see the psychiatrist one time. We just looked at each other. I grinned and said, "Well, he knew we were both crazy right off, so there was no need to waste his time on us." She agreed with me and we never told anyone anything different.

Company 7, TI (Technical Instructor) had been an Admirals aide before she came to Bainbridge. We were her first Company and I understand that she often talked about us to her future Companies. We never won a flag and actually missed one liberty because she over-reacted to something. She asked her Admiral to review the troops when we graduated, and he agreed. Bainbridge had never had an Admiral review a boot camp graduation, so everyone was excited. They decided since the graduation was in May, it should be done in white uniforms.

Normally, after the graduation ceremony, the graduating company leaves Bainbridge for leave to go home and prepare for their next duty station. Half of Company 7 made up half of the drill team. Armed Forces Day was a few days later and the drill team had been invited to perform at the US Army Aberdeen Proving Grounds, Maryland on Armed Forces Day in a U.S. Army Parade Ceremony. The powers that be decided to hold all of Company 7 over till after Armed Forces Day.

A week before graduation, the Drill Team Instructor, the Drill Instructor, our TI, the Recruit Drill Team Leader, the Recruit Company Commander and myself as Right Guide, all went to a meeting on the Parade Field. The Army marched on grass while the Navy usually marched on blacktop. The Army had gallon can lids hammered into the grass to show where the groups should stand and follow when they pass in review.

There was a high-ranking Army officer doing the talking. I did not know the Army ranks, but I could tell he was high-ranking by the way all other officers and enlisted paid close attention to everything he said. Toward the end he said, "And you Right Guides had better keep on those lids and stay in LINE!"

This had my three instructors turn and look at me – which had everyone there look at me! That senior Army officer grinned and said directly to me, "My guess is you are the Right Guide?" I answered in the only way one did in response to a question like that. A very respectful, "Yes Sir"!

We really looked great out there on Armed Forces Day 1959 in our white uniforms on the green grass and the Army units in green and tan. The Drill Team performed, then came back alongside the company. We dressed up without any missed steps. The rest of the drill team formed a unit behind us and shortly after was pass in review.

We received a lot of cheering and applause. As we marched off, the Chief told me to march all the way to the busses. There, soldiers were calling out for addresses. Dozens of people were taking pictures on the front and sides of the busses. The Recruit Company Commander was afraid of the crowd and wanted to stop. I told her to keep going; they would get out of our way. We had orders to go to the busses and if she stopped, I would run her over.

My dad's recruiting duty had ended. He and mom were able to come to the graduation and parade. Since recruits have to salute Chiefs as well as Officers, Dad said he gave and returned more salutes in those few days than in his whole 27-year career.

My next duty station was NAS Brunswick, ME. My test scores were not high enough to get A-school, so I was sent there to receive OJT (On the Job Training) as an Aviation Storekeeper. My roommate Marie had also been in Company 7 and was my bunk mate for the first few days of boot camp. She was assigned to OJT in the education office and found out you could still go TDY to A-school. Shortly after getting to Brunswick, she went off to school. When she returned she helped me go to A-school at NTTC, Memphis, TN.

Because I had been in OJT, Memphis could not put me on kitchen or barracks duty like normal; they had to start me on the Airman course. I already had my Airman stripes, but they still made me take the course. This meant I had to pass every test. Aviation Storekeeper School started every four weeks. I did three weeks of barracks duty instead of the normal 3 months. Also, the gals in charge of the enlisted school barracks were two who had been in Company 7 in boot camp.

Most of the WAVES had been the Valedictorian's and Salutatorians' of their high school graduating class and were going to electronic schools. I graduated 42nd in a class of 84, yet suddenly found myself in a leadership position. Some of the gals were shocked that the new girl was in charge.

In the Military, the one with the most rank is in charge in most cases. Some of the gals griped behind my back but one of them came to me after a couple days and said that she thought I was a blessing for her in a way. All her life, any goal she had ever set for herself, she had achieved. Not being put in the leadership position had made her realize that in life you don't always get what you want! I always respected her for having the fortitude to say that to my face while the others griped behind my back. I will say it was a three-month adventure being 19 and in charge of 50 women who were 18 – 21 years old. An entire book could possibly come out of that if, in my old age, I could remember it all. Maybe It is better not to tell all. One thing I do remember, is my future husband was there in Memphis, and he remembers seeing me march the gals of our unit to school each day.

After I returned to NAS Brunswick, ME in May, I worked in Base Supply taking care of P2V Neptune Aircraft parts. I met and married my husband, Les, on Armed Forces Day. We were in uniform and married in the Naval Chapel there. In those days, the day they knew you were pregnant they could force you out of the military. But if you were married and they needed you, they would let you stay until you started showing. Les was deployed with VP-21 and I asked to be released on my 21st birthday. A number of men got out on their 21st birthday; they used to call it a Kiddie Cruise. I would have stayed in if I could, but back then a congressman proposed a law that passed that said if a woman had a child in her home, regardless if it was her child or not, she had to get out of the service. That did not change until the 1970's when a woman officer took the issue to the Supreme Court.

I became a stay-at-home mom for 16 years. I had 4 kids, boy, girl, boy, girl. I was a volunteer at school, PTA, Cub Scouts, Girl Scouts, and Learning Disabilities. I could fill another book with those adventures! Les had never wanted me to work outside the home. However, in the mid-70's he came home one day and said, "Either you are going to have to get a job or we are going to have to stop eating!" I checked and found out I had 8 months left on my GI Bill and I could not only claim myself, but I could claim him and the kids. I went to junior college and took some courses to brush up on my office skills. Les got out of work for a short time and I got a work study Job. While at college, I ran into a US Army female recruiter and found out I was not too old to rejoin the service and they no longer had the limit on having children.

Les and I sat down at age 35 and decided we needed to find jobs that had retirements before we got much older. That meant government jobs.

I finished my Associate's Degree in three years. My husband Les got his Associate a year later. I joined the Oklahoma Air National Guard as a part-time traditional Guardsman. I was 36 years old and after about five tries, I got on as a full time OKANG Air Technician in Base Supply. In the meantime, Les had also given up a Computer Programing Job and took a $100 a month cut in pay to get on in maintenance to work on the C-130A model aircraft they had at the time. Those and the P2V's we worked with in the Navy were both made by Lockheed Martin and much of the equipment was the same. Les had been to schools on some equipment that no one at the Air Guard had ever been to. After all those years we both got straight across in our rate and pay. We had to take the Air Force courses and learn to speak Air Force instead of Navy.

When you are an Air Technician, you are accepted into Civil Service. However, you are still required to wear the Air Force uniform and be in the Air Guard militarily. If, for any reason, you lose your military positions you also lose your accepted Civil Service position 30 days later. After 20 years in the Air National Guard, the powers that be can force you to retire with the exception of a few critical Job codes.

For Example:

When my youngest daughter graduated from high school she joined the OKANG also. She was a traditional Air Guardsman for 5 years, occasionally doing temporary positions. Then she got a chance to get a full-time job as an OK Army National Guard Technician in computer security and she took it. At 39 with 22 years' service, she was forced to retire so they could use her slot. This could be used for enlisted or officer when the unit was going to Iraq and her position was not supposed to go. Since she could not retire due to her age and her MOS was critical, she was placed on priority placement and eventually got a regular civil service position at Tinker AFB.

After Spending a couple of years in base supply, I transferred into maintenance. The office was called Maintenance Supply Liaison or MSL. One of the guys made a sign that read "Momma Stotler's Lounge". It was up for a couple of years until a new commander got nervous because we had an off-base inspection team coming.

The supply and maintenance inspectors did not really know what all I was supposed to do. In addition, when they rewrote the National Guard Regulation, they left out two pages of my duties by accident. Because of this, I received a satisfactory on any inspection. It took 8 years for them to correct the National Guard Regulation.

A friend back east picked up on the missing pages and warned me not to dispose of the old regulation copy, so I had kept mine. One time one of the inspectors just had a hand-written page that someone told him was supposed to be our duties. When I told him there was more to it, he asked how I knew. I pulled out my old personal copy. He asked why I had it and if he could get a copy. He said that it would help him in his future inspections and he thanked me. One of our quality control folks went to a meeting where they updated regulations and I sent copies of how the regulation should have read. He said he submitted it and about a year later and the pages were reinstated. Not sure if my pushing corrected the problem but I was just glad to see it fixed.

We supported Volant Oak in Panama and I got to go on some of those rotations. Volant Oak supported the Embassies in Central and South America. I don't remember exactly how many times I went, but it was around 8 or 10 times. From time to time I got to go on one of the trips as mission essential ground personnel. Some trips would be to countries down and back in the same day. A few times I got to stay overnight in one of those countries. Les also went on these rotations, but we never went together; partly because if a plane crashed there would be no one to look after the kids.

One year, several officer families went with us to stay the night. They planned to do Christmas shopping. I had never been to Ecuador before. There was a lot of bad stuff going on there around that time. It must have been a slow or safer day because they let us go into the airport by climbing the luggage conveyor. Some folks in the USA tend to think of South American countries as backward, but this was a beautiful airport with a mall of high-dollar stores. When we left, another family joined us. In the course of the trip I heard the gentleman tell the loadmaster that he worked at the embassy and he wanted to get the family out to a safer area for a couple of weeks; that the kids were having to go to school in armored cars with guard cars as escorts.

After spending the night in Ecuador, we left with a heavy load not only a lot of shopping but a load of metal pallets. We had also picked up a few more 'space available' (Space A) passengers. One of the "Space A" officers, who should have known better, was letting his kid move around the plane on take-off. Since we were so crowded, the extra crew was braced in the back of the C-130H by the pallets. This kid came back to me and asked, "Is this plane going to make it?" I told him "Oh yes, Betsy will make it every time!" He said, "Is that the plane's name?" I said, "Yes, that is what her crew chief calls her. You should sit down." He did, but he popped right back up and came back and said, "Should we jettison part of the cargo?" A voice behind me said "KIDS FIRST!" He went back to his dad and told him, and we got a really dirty look! But his dad made him sit down and buckle up. I looked over my shoulder and saw a young enlisted man from operations behind me. My thought is he will go far.

Sure enough, after I retired I learned he made Colonel.

On another rotation, I got the chance to go on a four-country trip to Central America. Our first stop was in El Salvador, this was during their war. Again, the plane was really loaded with items for the various embassies. We had one female passenger and three men. We did not ask, but most of us figured they were CIA.

I was riding in the cockpit on the crew bunk. I noticed that the runway was lined with pillboxes manned with machine guns and squads. As we approached the airport terminal there were a couple dozen aircraft and about 20 guards with automatic weapons at each aircraft. The station manager not only had a radio on his hip, but was also armed with a .45.

They said only the pilot, co-pilot and navigator could leave the plane. I asked the pilot if it was possible for them to take me and the female passenger to a bathroom because the way the plane was loaded they could not drop the honey bucket. After the station manager, who is hired by the Embassy to take care of American aircraft, took the crew members to the operations department he came back and took me and the other lady to his office in a side building. I was able to get a good look up and down that ramp and could tell they were expecting trouble.

We unloaded a couple of the male passengers and some cargo but did not hang around long. I could tell the crew guys, most of whom were Vietnam combat veterans, breathed a bit easier when we got well away from there. Some years later, I went into to that same airport. The pillboxes were still there but not manned. They parked our C-130H a good city block away from the terminal and we walked there on our own. There were just 2 guards in the terminal half asleep. It was an interesting contrast.

Our next stop was Honduras. There was a USAF plane that looked like one of the Air Force Two aircraft by its paint job. A couple of US Army Helicopters landed not too far away on the ramp while we were there unloading items. The chopper pilot came running over because he saw "OKLAHOMA" down the side of the plane. He was from southeast Oklahoma and said it was so good to hear someone talking normal. A bunch of men who were in suits with cameras had gotten off the choppers and were getting on the Air Force Two type plane. One of the guys asked what was going on. The pilot said, "Oh, they are taking Jesse Jackson and a bunch of news guys on a grand tour for some reason."

We spent the night in Guatemala before flying to Costa Rica. Just as we got there and parked, there was that Air Force Two plane taking off and we learned they had stayed the night there. When we arrived back at Howard AFB Panama, there was that plane again. The next day it was gone. A couple days later our rotation was over and the second night home the news was saying something about Jesse Jackson having gone to Cuba and secured the release of an American prisoner. The news indicated the President was not happy with him going there, but since all had ended well, they would not charge him for going to Cuba.

Now there were at least 20 news people that got off those 2 choppers. I saw that plane in Honduras, Costa Rico and Panama. It was a blue, gray and white plane like the Air Force Two planes back then. Basically, the same paint job they have today, and nobody knew that Jesse Jackson was going or went to Cuba. Give me a break!

All in all, in my Oklahoma Air Guard career, I got to visit 18 countries. Some visits were brief, others I was able to stay a while. Since I was older when I went in, I had a lot of trouble with the weight control program. They wanted me to weigh what I weighed at 19, before giving birth to 4 kids, and most active duty retire in their 40's. Weight is a much bigger deal in peace time than in war time. I was basically forced out three days before my 58th birthday. I ended up with about 26 years combined in the Navy, Air Guard and the Ready Reserve. I still think it was a good day when I saw that "lady sailor" when I was 10 years old; which was 67 years ago.

There were other small adventures in what I think has been a very good life. I got to share that life with my soul mate for 54 years and 10 months to the day, when he went to the Leading Chief Topside. We camped, rode motorcycles, and 4-Wheelers in the great divide. I helped build the WIMSA (Women in Military Service for America) Memorial in a small way and got to go to the ground-breaking and dedication. I had a very small role in the Vietnam Women's Memorial Project and went to its dedication. This helped me receive the honor of being named "1993 Oklahoma Female Veteran of the Year".

I learned to quilt after my retirement, and have donated many of the 400 or so quilts I have made to military and civil causes as gifts or fundraisers. I never really had a "bucket list" as some people call it, like wanting to bungie jump, seems really dumb to me. I do wish I would have gone "Down Under" back when I could move better than I can now.

My family grew to 6 grandkids and one great grandchild. With a couple of son-in-laws and daughter-in-laws that brought in other extended family and friends who have been closer than family. By pure chance in 1992, at the 50th anniversary of the USN WAVES at the WAVES National Convention in California, I ran into my bunk mate "Cowboy" from Navy boot camp. But that's another story!

Katherine J.P. Stotler, TSgt, Retired

JUDITH KAUTZ, COL.
UNITED STATES AIR FORCE

The postcard arrived in May 1977 with a notice to respond within 24 hours or forfeit my selection for Air Force Officer Training School (OTS). It stated that my designated specialty would be Aircraft Maintenance. Wait! That wasn't one of my preferred options! I shouldn't have been surprised though, because that was the year the Air Force began accepting women into security forces, as well as aircraft and missile maintenance. I decided to accept and tough it out!

My husband, an Air Force Major at the time, administered my oath of enlistment. I tried to prepare myself physically and mentally for the challenge of attending OTS as an almost 30-year-old recruit. The experience taught me to endure 6-mile runs every day, humiliating comments by Flight Captains, and to march everywhere we went, among other things.

I graduated and got my commission two weeks before my 30th birthday, with my husband once again administering my oath. After a couple of weeks of leave, I headed off to Aircraft Maintenance Officer training. I spent several months learning about the principles of aerodynamics, engines, hydraulic and electrical systems on aircraft, as well as the significance of airpower in relation to the other services. The technical aspects were daunting to this newly-commissioned aircraft maintenance officer who had majored in English in college!

A Woman in a Man's World

My first assignment was to the 416th Organizational

Maintenance Squadron back at Griffiss AFB, New York, where I joined my husband at the base where he was currently assigned. And then my struggles began - not only to learn the business of maintaining the huge B-52 Bombers and KC-135 Tankers (air refueling aircraft,) but to deal with the issues of adapting to an environment that was male-dominated, where women weren't welcome. Although there were many challenges, let me highlight three we confronted as women in a man's world.

First, of particular concern were the enlisted men who dominated the aircraft maintenance career fields. Many were disgruntled and frustrated, commenting often how we made it more difficult for them to do their jobs. Many of the young enlisted women entering the career field couldn't carry the tool boxes, or even use the tools because of their small hands. It also wasn't unusual to see these young women dragging vehicle chocks (used behind the wheels of vehicles to keep them stationary) so they could reach the aircraft entry doors. As a result, the men often had to shoulder more of the work to make up for what the women couldn't do, which understandably led to resentment and anger, and ultimately drove many men to unprofessional behavior.

The tool issue created a major hardship for both men and women in aircraft maintenance. The situation got so difficult that the Air Force launched a major study of tools and tool boxes. After a few years and through much testing and evaluation, tools were redesigned so that they could easily be used in smaller hands with the same or better efficiency as old tools. Additionally, tool boxes were also resized, and they were made of lighter material to reduce the total weight of the box filled with tools. And guess what? Everyone benefitted from the changes! The re-engineering of these tools, which was so vital to the basics of the aircraft maintenance career field, might never have occurred if women hadn't joined this specialty. What an improvement in efficiency for everyone!

The second challenge was bathrooms, which created hardships on women (and men), even lasting throughout a good part of my thirty years in the Air Force. At first, there were unisex bathrooms, where a sign indicated if the facility was occupied, and it was labeled front and back for men or women. The conditions were crude and often filthy, and it seemed no one cleaned up after themselves. Most times it was easier, although time-consuming, to trek from the flight line to the hangar administrative areas where bathrooms were better. It was not pleasant to see the dirty looks at daily roll call and listen to announcements about keeping the bathrooms clean. Cleaning latrines added extra tasks to the challenging work of getting aircraft prepared for flight and repaired when they returned from daily missions.

Eventually, the reality that women were here to stay set in, and the service began to construct or improve bathroom facilities in aircraft maintenance hangars. But progress was slow, and even after I spent ten years in the Air Force, I still worked in facilities where latrines were unisex. I found it so humiliating to have to walk down the bathroom entry hall and shout, "Is anybody in there?" before I could use the facility. That may seem silly to some, but in a career field where women were watched constantly to see how we performed, it just added to the pressure of the job.

In this day and age of women deploying alongside men in every career field, these issues don't seem to bother anyone. As a Colonel the last year I served before retirement, I deployed to the Middle East, and lived on an Army base in an undisclosed country. Our quarters were 8 by 16-foot trailers, stacked on top of each other on concrete floors in a large building. Although I did have my own trailer, I shared a gang latrine with all the other female inhabitants of the building. My trailer was 156 steps from the latrine (I counted them!) and I still found it humiliating to trek from my trailer to the facility in my pajamas, because I often encountered those folks who worked for me. However, it didn't seem to bother them. It seems that young military members have a different mindset from those of us who paved the way for women's entry into non-traditional career fields. They take conditions in stride, knowing that there may be enemies around every corner, and all other issues seem unimportant. I still believe that ultimately, the presence of women in these non-traditional career fields resulted in conditions that were better for everyone.

Surprisingly enough, I thrived in the hostile environment of aircraft maintenance and took on each new challenge with determination and resolve. But interestingly enough, one of the third challenging issues throughout my career was the uniform.

We were required to wear a utility uniform – in those

days, they were called fatigues – because our blue uniform was certainly not conducive to work around airplanes, aerospace ground equipment and their respective fluids. Initially, there were no women's utility uniform, so we had to wear male fatigues. For me as well as most women, it meant purchasing trousers and shirts that buttoned on the wrong side and were miles too big. The shirt pockets came down to my waist and the trouser pockets almost to my knees! Every uniform required some modifications, but fortunately, I was an adept seamstress! Once I purchased a new uniform, I had to remove the shirt cuffs, shorten the sleeves, and then sew the cuffs back on. The trousers weren't exactly suited to the female figure, so they had to be modified as well. And, since it was mandatory to wear protective shoes in aircraft maintenance, finding steel-toed boots that fit meant wearing small men's sizes – for me, it was a size 4 ½.

In a couple of years, we were presented with a female utility uniform with disastrous results. The blouse had pockets that were so small our identification cards wouldn't even fit in them. Name tapes and the USAF tapes that went over the tops of the pockets were so long they extended under the arm! Instead of the shirt tucking in as the men's did, it had slits on the side, so we had to wear it on the outside. This frustrated us because it set us aside from the men even more! The trouser pockets were extremely small, and the waist was tiny in proportion to the rest of the trousers. We dealt with all these uniform challenges as we grappled with trying to work in a man's career field. Eventually, after we struggled for a few more years, they produced a utility uniform which allowed us to function on the flight line, and even finally created a maternity utility uniform and a flight suit as well.

The Role of Mentoring

Mentoring others plays an important role, no matter what the career – military or civilian – but never was it more important than when women entered non-traditional jobs in the Air Force. There were many who offered me mentorship during my career, from enlisted members to commanders, both male and female. But in the 1970s when we were just beginning our journey as aircraft maintainers, there weren't many women supervisors. In fact, in most organizations where I served I was the only woman officer. We were constantly evaluated to see if we could do the job, and we often felt like we had to do twice as well as our male counterparts to be considered half as good. It was in this environment where mentorship was so important.

The organizational structure of an aircraft maintenance squadron included branches that usually maintained specific weapon systems, and each branch was directed by an officer, Lieutenant or Captain depending on the size of the branch, and a senior enlisted supervisor. Pairing branch leaders in this way allowed maintenance officers in training to experience the benefits of enlisted supervisors who had served for at least 15 years. The men I was paired with were superb for the most part, with rare exceptions and they truly set the example for subordinates. I learned so much about the specific aircraft assigned to the branch as well as techniques for supervising, especially enlisted people. Most of them treated me with respect and patience; of course, this also demanded that I acted professionally and take a mature approach to learning.

Commanders played an important mentoring role by setting the example in their treatment of me. Of course, as female maintenance officers, we preferred being treated as equal to the men, with no special deference or privileges. This was difficult for some of our commanders, who often took on a fatherly role, calling us "honey" or "dear". Of course, this sent the wrong message to our fellow squadron members, who certainly believed we got special treatment. How many times did I have a private session with the boss, requesting that he not call me by those titles? (To this day, it rankles me to be called honey or dear by anyone except a member of my family!)

However, most of my commanders did everything they could to ensure I was afforded opportunities equal to my male counterparts. They sent me to professional military schools like Squadron Officer School and gave me assignments on temporary duty to other bases to carry out our mission. For example, when Mount St. Helens erupted in 1980, my duty station was Fairchild Air Force Base in Spokane, Washington, which was right in the path of the volcanic ash. It was determined that our aircraft couldn't take off or land with all the ash on the flight line, so it would have to be cleaned up. In order to continue our training missions for our crew members, we sent our aircraft accompanied by personnel to maintain them, to three other bases. I was selected to be Officer-In-Charge of the maintainers for four KC-135 tankers, as we deployed to Beale Air Force Base in northern California. I was proud to be chosen to lead the largest contingent. This was one example of mentorship where my commander provided me a great opportunity for leadership and learning.

I will never forget one particular incident where Colonel Mason, my Deputy Commander for Maintenance (DCM) and in charge of the entire aircraft maintenance complex, really demonstrated true mentorship. One of my responsibilities as Officer-In-Charge of Quality Assurance was the Foreign Object Damage program, which administered all the actions to prevent damage to aircraft engines through ingesting foreign objects.

Strategic Air Command, our base headquarters, sent out a message to quality assurance officers with some instruction which included the phrase, "Gentlemen, we must get this program under control." Being sensitive to equal treatment for women maintenance officers, I was extremely upset, so I marched into the DCM's office. I presented him the message and said, "I assume this doesn't apply to our office, since it isn't supervised by a gentleman." I stated how concerned I was that our command was not setting the example to include women. Instead of telling me to calm down and not worry about it, he took me seriously. He picked up the phone, called the originator of the message, and counseled him about the wording of his messages in the future to ensure they were gender neutral. What a wonderful example of mentorship! Through his actions, Colonel Mason told me women like me were an important part of the maintenance community, and he demonstrated an appropriate way to treat the situation.

As a woman maintenance officer, I also took on a lot of roles as mentor, especially to the young women enlisted members who were new to this challenging career field. Most had male supervisors who just didn't know how to deal with these young women. Many were challenged by menstrual cycles, which were further complicated by less than optimum bathroom facilities. Some women used their cycles as excuses not to work, which created further resentment among the men. Many women were harassed, both verbally and sexually, and were afraid to tell anyone, under the threat from their supervisors of being dismissed from the Air Force. Often, they didn't know how to act, which made it even more important for us to set an example for them. Later in my career, I was selected frequently to investigate accusations of harassment by supervisors, many of whom had never supervised women before. This afforded me even more opportunities to mentor.

I had the privilege of commanding two squadrons during my career, and commanding should be the epitome of mentoring. As commanders, we lived in a fishbowl – we were watched 24 hours a day. In fact, sometimes I believed the folks lurked under my bed because they knew so much about what went on in my life. This made it vitally important to set the example – as a leader, a mentor, and a woman. First, I chose a woman first sergeant, and together we were women leaders conducting our squadron's business. Additionally, I gladly served on court martial boards when called to do so, or, as mentioned above, as an investigating officer for cases of sexual misconduct or harassment.

Another one of our tasks as commanders was to serve administrative punishment to our subordinates. To mentor my supervisors and their subordinates after the administration of punishment, I gathered them along with the offender and together we discussed what options I had and why I chose the punishment I did. We talked about how the offender could recover, and what actions he/she would have to take to regain a meaningful career in the Air Force. In this way, my first sergeant and I set the example as a woman supervisor and commander. Feedback from squadron members was positive about this process of mentorship.

A Most Memorable Career

My 30 years in the Air Force were extremely challenging, yet extremely rewarding. I had the privilege of fielding four different types of aircraft into our Air Force inventory, including the B-1B bomber, the T-6A Texan II trainer, and two aircraft in the national VIP fleet at Andrews Joint Air Base: The C-37 Gulfstream V and the C-32 Boeing 757, commonly used as Air Force 2. The B-1B was brought back by President Reagan after the program was cancelled by President Carter and remains today a significant part of our bomber fleet.

The T-6A Texan II replaced the aging T37 as a trainer for both Air Force and Navy pilots going through pilot training. It brought greater efficiencies to the training program. The C37 Gulfstream V is one of the members of the small VIP Gulfstream fleet used to carry our national leaders to the places they need to go to conduct our country's business. Because these aircraft are smaller, they are more fuel efficient and their engines are more environmentally friendly. Finally, the C-32 was introduced to replace the 707s retired from the VIP fleet in the late 1990's. It is a large capacity aircraft which was modified to include a stateroom for leaders like the Vice President and Secretary of State. When it carries the Vice President, its assigned call sign is Air Force 2. These airplanes are all vital to our nation's defense and I am proud to have played a part in bringing them into service for the Air Force, where they continue to serve today.

As one of the first women in the aircraft maintenance career field, I believe I made a difference for those who followed. We fought for equal treatment in a man's world, while at the same time establishing our credibility as skillful members and leaders of the maintenance community. We endeavored to ensure those that followed had every opportunity to be trained, to lead and to command. We fought against harassment of all types, for both men and women, and strove to right the injustices committed against our fellow airmen. We worked alongside our male counterparts; long hours on frozen or torrid flight lines, enduring a myriad of conditions so we could get the aircraft launched on their vital missions. We did all this not for praise but because we knew it had to be done to keep our country safe.

I am so honored and privileged to have served my country for 30 years, and also gratified that jointly, my husband and I have contributed 57 years toward the defense of the United States. Moreover, together with my fellow aircraft maintenance officers, I know we improved conditions and opportunities for women to serve. I will always be a patriot and always proud to be an Air Force Veteran.

RENEE M. KATERI PEELER, SGT
UNITED STATES AIR FORCE

My interest in joining the Air Force first piqued when I accompanied my mom to see my older sister off into the Army. She was put up in a downtown hotel the night before she was to head off to boot camp. They shared rooms with other recruits and her roommate was a girl enlisting in the Air Force. I struck up a conversation with her and she told me the benefits of joining the Air Force, even on her first day and she was already recruiting for the Air Force. My dad, a former Marine, died when I was nine and mom raised six of us by herself. I knew she didn't have the money for me to go to college so when the recruiters came to the school in my senior year, the initial interest grew, and I was really asking questions. I visited the recruiting station where I was shown a list of jobs in the Air Force and their civilian related jobs. Airframe Mechanic had a nice ring to it, so I chose it. I was already mechanically inclined, so it was a natural fit.

I had to pass my physical and had never been to a gynecologist so that was my first of many new experiences. While my feet were still in the stirrups, the doctor pronounced I had flat feet. It was later determined that I didn't have flat feet and they let me in the service. I spoke to a neighbor with a similar experience and it was decided it must be something this doctor said as code if you were a virgin. I was only 17 when I graduated so I signed up for a delayed entry. I went to work over the summer at McDonald's until I was old enough to officially join the service.

I went to basic training at Lackland AFB in December of 1975 and attended technical school for large airframe aircraft at Chanute AFB. Tech school was kind of fun. I imagine it is a little like being in college. You have the dorm life, studying, and everyone hanging around with each other and yes the horse play which led to me cracking the end of my radius bone the day before block 3's final exam. I didn't know it was cracked and as I was trying to study it was throbbing so much I had a friend take me over to medical. It was taking so long I was afraid I was going to miss my test. However, I took the test on schedule and passed, but had to convince my instructor I could continue on with block 4 in my cast. I graduated with the rest of my class and was stationed at Anderson AFB in Guam.

I worked many aspects of the aircraft mechanic's job during my time in Guam, recovery crew, phase dock and my favorite as assistant crew chief. One of the things you have to do to prepare for flight is check the fuel gauges for accuracy. I would walk down the back bone of the B-52D lay on my belly and reach over, open the fuel tank and put the dip stick in the tank to get measurements, all without a harness. I guess it wasn't a safety concern back then, but I will say one thing, the dark camouflage paint job in the hot Guam sun will burn your arms when you wear a short sleeve shirt.

Another female airman approached me about creating an all-girl crew. I was sorry to disappoint her, but I was taking into consideration we worked on the B-52D aircraft. It has a 100+ pound drag chute to load. As a 5' 3" woman it was tough enough loading it with a guy let alone another woman. Also, I didn't think I had anything to prove because they used to get me to work the tight areas. It was give and take at least on my crew. I know it wasn't that way for everyone back then, but I was very blessed. It was a different culture back then and you had to filter out the noise.

There weren't many women in the maintenance field in 1976 and the maintenance hangar only had one bathroom, so you had to have someone stand guard, so the guys wouldn't walk in on you.

The fatigues back then were pretty heavy olive drab material and really didn't do anything for you as a female. I worked side by side with my crew chief and yet when I approached him and chatted with him in the NCO club in civilian clothes, it took 15 minutes before I saw a light bulb go off when he realized it was me talking to him.

You would think female airman would stand up for each other, and we should mentor each other in various ways, but I found out the hard way it isn't always the case. I would go eat lunch in my room and sometimes my boyfriend would come with me. Rooms were adjoined by the shared shower and bathroom. When a fellow airman would go in her room next door, you could hear her. I would shout over a greeting to her and he would grumble and not say nice things. I would say "Ruth" is nice, why do you want to talk about her? One day he finally got tired of me defending her and told me she had been passing around a rumor I was sleeping around. He said MSgt Van Camp called her in and said "Ruth" you know that isn't true and put a stop to it. I always was appreciative to MSgt Van Camp and glad someone looked out for the truth.

I was next stationed at Tinker AFB in 1978 working for the 552nd AWACS. They were in the process of writing the Technical Orders for the E-3As so some mechanics were farmed out to other positions and worked until I was honorably discharged in 1980. I was proud to serve and when I was discharged I was lucky enough to continue working for my country and get back to working on planes. Tinker AFB was hiring for aircraft mechanics, sheet metal mechanic, hydraulic specialists, and jet engine mechanics. The interview panel asked me what job I would like to work. I told them I know I have aircraft mechanic experience, but I would like to work sheet metal. I expressed it would be more like I was making something instead of just taking it apart and putting it back together. They hired me and sent me to the first class in the new on-base vocational technical school.

Things don't always fall in your lap. Just as I asked to work as a sheet metal mechanic I also had to ask to work on the aircraft instead of the back shop which I was scheduled to work after technical school. Part of our training was rotating through the various areas after we were trained in the classroom. I knew from the time in the back shop I would be working one part over and over and I wanted to learn a variety of skills and jobs on the aircraft. I was told if I could get someone to swap with me and both supervisors to agree, I could switch. It wasn't hard finding a volunteer to switch, but the aircraft supervisor took some convincing to accept me as he wasn't fond of women workers.

I served my country through the Military and Federal service for 38 years and 7 months and would do it all over again.

KYM NELSON, SGT
UNITED STATES MARINE CORPS

1997. This was a year that would shape my life forever. It was the year I signed the dotted line and joined the Marine Corps. I was 17 years old and living in a small town. I was ready for a change. I was ready to find myself. My parents couldn't afford college and I had a choice; keep living there and continuing the road I was on or find something to get me up and out.

The day I met Staff Sergeant Marvin Best, I was a mess. I went to test for my ASVAB and was not in the right frame of mind. This man walked right up to me and showed me the extraordinary value of the Marines and this was a perfect fit for me. He told the Navy and Army recruiters to keep walking and we talked for an hour. From that day, I was determined to be a Marine. I went home and told my parents. While my mom cried and said no, my dad laughed and said yes. My sister was 7 at the time and couldn't fathom her big sister leaving.

In July 1998, I was off. I had spent 7 months in the Delayed Entry Program immersing myself in all of the activities and training available; running daily, conditioning, weekends with the recruiters working on knowledge, skills and other necessary tools for success. I learned so much and found myself feeling limitless and I was. Boot Camp wasn't easy mentally, but I found this voice that I had never heard before. The voice that told me to keep moving and keep climbing. I soon found myself on top of the world. I was happier than I had ever been. I was 17 when I graduated in October. My parents came to graduation along with my sister and saw me earn my place. I finally felt like I was doing something more than most kids my age.

My time in the Corps isn't much different from anyone

else. I worked hard. I earned everything I had. There wasn't a time anything was ever handed to me. I served, I became a mother and a friend, but most of all, I became a leader. I don't believe there is anything in this world that can stop a person other than their own mindset. I saw that a lot while I was in. One of the most important lessons I learned was to always be who I am. Never let anything take who I am away and never to lose myself. And that has stuck with me through my time out of the Corps. While not always easy, there have been times I have struggled. I have dug deep and found the intestinal fortitude to never allow anything to define who I am. These are lessons that I am teaching my children.

It's been 13 years since I left the Corps, but the values and the lessons are still ingrained deep in my soul. I have found more of a struggle in civilian life than I ever thought I would. I walked out to a world I thought would appreciate people like me who are hard charging and driven. Often times I find myself questioning the civilian life and how people can live their lives without accountability and discipline. I find a moral compass issue with people scratching and clawing their way to a promotion, rather than working as a team. I have fought tooth and nail to try and change perceptions. Often times I am told to slow down and not care so much. I will never understand this mentality. If there is any take away I could hand off to employers, it is to appreciate your Veterans for the work ethic and experience they come with. While we aren't always fun or easy to work with, we have a mission and a drive. We want to take the team with us on our journey. We don't always take credit for the work we do and when we do it's often because we are cleaning up a large mess that someone left before us. We will work as a team, but you must be hungry to learn from us, too. You cannot expect us to stop what we are doing (because we are on a mission) to train you and seek you out; we want you to want it. Nothing is ever given in this life. There is a satisfaction that comes with leading a team and watching your groups engage and learn.

I believe that there is not a more employable person than that of a Marine. We have learned many lessons in our time. Everything about us is different and we are cut from a cloth that is unlike any other. We are taught respect, how to learn and often times take responsibility for things that others will not. Often times taking responsibility for things where we are not at fault or have direct control over. We don't always do or say the popular things and we pay for it by losing people in our lives. We are viewed as abrasive and brash. We control our emotions most of the time. We set goals and smash them. I personally have my "kill list" which is a compilation of all of the tasks I need to accomplish for the day. I put it together each morning/afternoon and check each one off as I work through them. We are a dedicated breed and are not manipulated by the façade that is often times put in our path. We lead with passion and undying dedication to those around us, to include our leaders. We have a sense of pride in everything that we do and face. We walk taller and are confident because of it. We have been taught to learn. Not just learn a little, but everything that goes along with the task. We work to be the best and to bring others to the same level. We know our job, the job of others, and our boss's job. We take a tremendous amount of pride in our reputation and can come off as egotistical, but we are not. We are compassionate and humble with a great love for ourselves, our family, our country, and her people. We understand being a part of something bigger than ourselves.

If there is anything that I could give to anyone reading this, it is this: Everyone has "shit". Everyone goes through things. It is up to you how you respond and how you face those situations. I will never allow anything or anyone to define me. I will never allow someone or something to DEFINE ME. I do not "fit" in the social norms and I never will. I free think and have learned from everything I have ever been through in my life. While this excerpt is a VERY small portion of my life and my heart, know that I have been through things too. I am not a victim. I am a fighter, I am strong, and I am a Marine. The oath doesn't stop the day you leave your active service. You continue to share experiences and help people shape and grow. There is nothing more satisfying than watching your team link arms and grow with you; watching your team flourish. This continues as a parent. Choices and reactions come with consequences or rewards. My children learn these values. I will ensure they carry these values for all of their life and to hand those values down through the generations.

There isn't anything extraordinary about me. I am a Marine. I am a mother. I work for the best aerospace company in the world. I have an incredibly wonderful man in my life that continues to push me to be better than I was yesterday. I don't have a lot of "friends". Mostly acquaintances. Trust is something that is hard pressed to earn from me. And I will let you know when I am disappointed or proud of you. I am black and white. There isn't much room for grey area. I tell it like it is. I stand up for the little guy. I fight for the good of the team. I can see a bigger picture than most and I make decisions on a dime (yet can't figure out what the hell I want for dinner). I resonate with pride and expect others to be accountable for themselves. But most of all, I am me. I am extraordinary.

LISA JACKSON
UNITED STATES ARMY

I could say that I had always aspired to be in the military or that it was some childhood dream, but the truth is it was just a means to an end. I grew up in a small town, as the name suggests, called Flat River, Missouri. I was 19 years old at this point and had lived a very sheltered life as far as seeing the outside world. In fact, I had only left the state of Missouri to visit my family in Arkansas. I fumbled my way through high school not really applying myself, more focused on surviving through years of child abuse and finding a way to escape the hell that I had lived through.

The military was that escape. I took my enlistment oath at the MEPS center in St. Louis, Missouri. After enlisting, I snuck outside briefly to smoke a couple puffs on a cigarette. I put my half-smoked cigarette in the butt can, only to be shocked as a homeless man dug it back out, put it in his mouth, and asked me to light it. I had never seen a homeless person before. I lit our cigarette per his request and gave him a few more cigarettes since I couldn't take them with me.

My first Army job I signed for was a still photographer. I was very excited but also afraid of the unknown at the same time. I had taken my oath but wasn't scheduled to leave for a few months and I had barely passed on the military weight standards. By the time I was ready to ship out, I had purposely sabotaged myself and gained weight by eating nothing but bananas and cheeseburgers and no longer met the weight standard. My whole contract had to be renegotiated and I was told since I had taken my oath I wouldn't be able to get out of my contract with the Army. I lost the few pounds that I needed to lose and was given a new job. My new MOS was an 88M, which was a truck driver. I was told that I would be driving generals around because I was a female and I of course didn't think that the recruiters would ever lie to me, so I accepted the Army's generous offer.

Next thing I knew I was on an airplane to Newark, New Jersey, to Fort Dixx. I had never been on an airplane before. Everything looked microscopic and I was amazed at the big world that was out there waiting for me to discover it. I felt this was my getaway and that I was finally free of the emotional chains that bound me. I was ready to embrace whatever lie ahead of me. It couldn't be any worse than where I had come from.

My freedom that I felt on the airplane was short lived. At basic training in-processing, we were told to stand in line and empty all our pockets. Next, we were filling out mounds of paperwork as orders were barked at us. After that I was rushed to receive my TA50, which consisted of two duffle bags and a ruck sack full of BDU's, military long johns, wet weather gear, MOPP (Mission Oriented Protective Posture) gear, which included a gas mask, and a sleeping bag. After being issued all of this equipment, we were marched to reception. Not only did we have to carry our military bags, but also our civilian bags. I wondered how in the hell I was expected to carry all of this stuff, but it was obvious that I didn't have any choice in the matter. On top of that, I had no rhythm and couldn't stay in step with the left-right-left thing as we marched. I was on left when they were marching on right. I felt like Private Benjamin minus the blonde hair!

Next was reception that lasted about four days, and you had to be able to do at least one push-up to start basic training. I had a room with eight other females. The room was nothing but walls of bunkbeds and wall lockers. It was my first actual taste of what the military was like. Wake-up was at 0500 every morning and we marched everywhere. Our beds had green wool blankets that were itchy and hideous to look at along with white sheets, a pillow, and pillow case. The beds had to be made hospital style. The corners of the blanket had to be folded at a 45-degree angle with the blankets so tight against the bed that a quarter could bounce off the corner. Every morning we had inspections and if our beds weren't made right, they were ripped apart and we had to start all over. Our wall lockers had to be Dress Right, DRESS and we had to have a spit shine on our boots, which was not an easy skill to master.

We were issued field manuals that were supposed to tell us everything about the Army. We had to learn the rank structure and call everyone by their appropriate rank as well as stand at parade rest or attention. When we went to the chow hall we had to stand at parade rest to eat and never had enough time to finish our food. It was like taking cake from the fat kids. After four days in reception, I still couldn't do a correct push-up, so I was sent to a place called FITCO. I began to panic: "What if I can't do this?" In order to get out of FITCO and move onto basic training, I would have to build my upper body strength by lifting weights and be able to do twelve push-ups. FITCO was actually better than I expected. People everywhere I went seemed to really like me, which really built my confidence in that regard. FITCO was co-ed and some of the men were really cute, but I wasn't attracted to them because they didn't have any upper body strength. After two weeks, I was able to do the minimum number of pushups and was sent on to basic training with some other girls that had given me the nickname of "Smiley."

Once again, we packed all our gear and bags and marched across post and I, still not knowing my left foot from my right, was trying not to stick out since I couldn't march. Upon arriving for basic there were eight drill sergeants all barking orders and yelling social security numbers. When we heard the last four numbers of our social security number, we were supposed to go to them, and then we would be in their company. The problem was that all eight of them were yelling numbers at the same time. They called my number three times before I realized that it was mine, because apparently, I had forgotten my social. I fell out of formation only to see four of them coming towards me like bats out of hell. I felt the tears swelling in my eyes and wanted to run for the hills, but there I stood, motionless. All of the drill sergeants started yelling at me, asking me what was wrong with my hearing, and did I have something wrong with me. I don't even remember what else they said. After this fiasco, we were all taken by the drill sergeants to our building, which was called a company. The company consisted of four platoons, twelve drill sergeants, and a senior drill sergeant. There were about forty girls in my platoon and five in my room. I felt left out because I currently didn't have a ranger buddy while everyone else did. After a few days we got a new girl; her name was Ebert. Later during physical training formation that evening, I heard someone start to sneeze and when I looked over I saw Ebert sneeze all over the person in front of her, who wasn't aware or was too afraid to move from attention. No one seemed to notice but Ebby and me, so now we had our own secret. After that she and I started talking and decided to become ranger buddies. Ebert, who I called Ebby, was one of the funniest people I had ever met.

Basic was even harder than I had expected--it was

emotionally and physically exhausting. The first two weeks of basic were the hardest. We had at least ten formations a day, marched everywhere, and didn't get much sleep. We were going through basic in the winter in New Jersey, where the wind felt like it could cut through you and it seemed to rain every day.

Ebby helped me a lot because she kept me motivated and moving, which also kept me warm. We made the best out of every situation. I remember one day it was raining, and we were told that we had five minutes to put on our wet weather gear and fall back out into formation. I had all my gear on except I couldn't get one of my over boots on. Ebby tried to help me. I had one leg up in the air and she was straining to put my boot on with all her might. She was pushing so hard that her hair pinned up by bobby pins started falling down. She became so impatient that she threw my leg into the wall which made both of us fall down as we laughed hysterically and then somehow magically got my over boot on just in time for formation.

Ebby and I became very close. When she got dropped for push-ups, I dropped to the ground with her and vice versa. The drill sergeants began to refer to us as Frick and Frack. Drill sergeants from other classes started talking to us because they thought we were hilarious, while our drill sergeants rode us hard. Ebby and I always got in trouble for talking and with all the push-ups we had to do, we were in pretty good shape.

I remember one time, my drill sergeant asked everyone to tell their first names and where they were from. When it was my turn, I stated that I was from Missouri. My drill sergeant starting yelling at me and telling me that I wasn't from Missouri and after repeated, unsuccessful attempts to convince him that I was from Missouri, I shouted Texas. Every time my drill sergeant asked me where I was from, I said something different; to me, it had just become a game and each time I said something different it made him even madder. In my mind, I felt like I was in control and this was a fun game that I was finally going to win. I didn't think it was funny any longer when he released everyone back into the building except me. I spent the next several hours with two drill sergeants dogging me with pushups, jumping jacks, and low crawls through mud, and those two drill sergeants simultaneously yelling different commands and expecting me to do both. I was ready to break, but I held in the tears and was determined that I wouldn't quit. When I was finally released to go inside, I was covered in mud and completely exhausted. The girls told me how proud they were of me; I was proud of myself too.

It was the drill sergeant's job to break you down and then build you back up or break you until you quit. After that incident it seemed as if the drill sergeants were picking on me, but as long as I had the support of Ebby and the girls I could make it.

Ebby had long hair and during physical training some of her hair would fall down and the drill sergeants would yell at her. So every time I caught them not looking I would pin her hair back up with extra bobby pins I kept in my pockets. Ebby and I were an invincible team. We even pulled guard duty together. When Ebby had guard duty I would stay up with her and talk to her during her shift and vice versa. One night, because I had told her that I would pull guard duty with her, she attempted to wake me up. I sat up straight in the bed like I was possessed and yelled, "Do what?" and started laughing hysterically; then I fell back asleep. She told me the next morning what had happened, and I didn't remember any of it. That incident became another shared story on our long list of secrets.

For Ebby's birthday I had stayed up the whole night before making items to decorate her bunkbed. She was so surprised; I think it made her realize how important she truly was to me. We conveniently had cupcakes for dessert at the chow hall that day. Ebby was on a duty and didn't go to chow with us. This would be a perfect opportunity to sneak her a surprise cupcake.

I wrapped a cupcake in a napkin and stole it out of the chow hall to surprise her for her birthday. I held onto that smashed cupcake in my pocket for what seemed like hours. I looked for Ebby after chow and she wasn't anywhere in sight, so I did the most reasonable thing and ate the cupcake. Immediately after I devoured this cupcake, I was told that Ebby was looking for me. It was like she knew. So there it is--I had betrayed my friend by eating her celebratory birthday cupcake because the Army was starving me. To make up for this, I had developed a plan. What girl doesn't like chocolate? Either because I was sneaky, wanted to see what I could get by with, or just plain stupid, I would sneak to the PX and buy candy bars and then hide them in the hedge bushes outside our company, until we could sneak back outside to eat them. By this time Ebby and I had also gotten close to another girl who we would share the candy bars with; she was named Pittman.

We had been at basic training for four weeks now and Christmas was around the corner, so we had a break in training called Christmas Exodus. On Christmas Exodus we were allowed to fly home in our Class A Uniform for a two-week break. I didn't mind wearing my dress uniform because I was so proud of myself for making it this far. Ebby wanted me to go home on leave with her. But I knew I needed to go home to Missouri because I missed my brother and worried about how my mother was treating him. My mom, brother, and grandparents were waiting at the airport to greet me. I really missed my brother and started crying when I saw his little face. I guess I had even missed my mother to some degree and hoped she would respect me and treat me better.

My mother took me to all of my relatives' houses and had me show them how I could do push-ups, just like the men had to do. She even allowed me to drive her car. This was the first time that I drove my mother's car and truly felt that she was proud of me. I spent a lot of time with my brother and even helped decorate the Christmas tree.

Christmas came and went, just like my leave. It was time to fly back to New Jersey to finish the last four weeks of basic training. I was dreading going back, except I had really missed Ebby and my new-found friends. When we returned, we all exchanged stories of the things that we had done while on leave.

By January it was still freezing in New Jersey, but Ebby and I stayed highly motivated by making up our own cadences to sing. The next month consisted of M-16 ranges, FTX field problems, and the gas chamber. We spent the next four weeks wearing our cavalier helmets, which made us feel like we were ninja turtles.

Finally, it was time to enter the legendary gas chamber.

The gas chamber was very scary; it was actually a building and the only way to get in or out was if the drill sergeants opened the door. Once again, we were at their mercy. Ebby and I held hands as we watched the first row go through the chamber, take off their masks, and recite their name and social, as they had been instructed to do by the drill sergeants. When the drill sergeants were sure that everyone had inhaled the gas, they opened the door. There was no way of faking your way out of this! One by one, once the gas entered their lungs, the others began coughing, crying, jumping up and down, and vomiting.

At first it was funny to watch. They all looked like lunatics waving their arms like birds, and I thought maybe they were just being overly dramatic; but then it was our turn. The door of the building opened, and we entered into the building in a line. The drill sergeants told us to break the seal of our masks and take them off. I tried to hold my breath as long as I could, but the gas filled up my lungs, and everything burnt including my skin. I was convinced that I was dying and could hardly see when the door came open. But, I could feel fresh air and ran towards it. I almost ran straight into a tree that seemed strategically placed in line with the door; I believed the drill sergeants had purposely placed it there.

Like all things in life, Basic training came to a bittersweet end and it was time for AIT (Advanced Individual Training). My AIT to become a truck driver was at Fort Dixx. Ebby was going to AIT at Fort Sam to be a field medic. Ebby and I vowed to be friends forever, and that if we ever had children and later died, we would raise the other one's kids. We loved and trusted each other that much! Our song was, and would always be, Bette Midler's "Wind Beneath My Wings."

NICKELETTE HUNTER, MSGT
UNITED STATES AIR FORCE

Divorce: Yes Please, with a Venti Vanilla Latte and a Double Shot of Makers Mark on the Side!!

Probably wasn't the title you were expecting, but hey, it's not your story ... it's mine. Before you start reading some words about real life, pour a glass of wine, kick back, and chill out. Life. Not always how we planned it out in our young minds, right? So.....Grow up, head off to college, sow some wild oats, party your ass off, land your dream job, finally meet the right fella, fall in love, get married, have some little ones, and settle into life. Well, some of you out there had the cash to get that big start in life and some of you did them out of order. Whatever the case, little girls dream about their wedding day and the life they will someday have. Shit. I know there are more than a few of you out there that have stepped in the mud holes of life, taken a few whacks to the shins, made at least a couple poor decisions, and even had some regret staring back at you in the mirror. Right? I can see you nodding as you read this. Let me be honest, life has molded you into who you are sitting here today. Your story that you are living out, could possibly be the encouragement or counseling some individual needs to hear 11 years from now. Relationships can be one of those bad life decisions or they can be the best thing to happen to you. I have learned some lessons in life... sometimes the hard way. Today, I have no regrets. You can, too. Why not? Divorce was one of the best things that happened for me. Life ain't perfect and if we expect it to be, then we're missing the whole point. By the way, my name is Nic, and when you're done with your first glass, pour another for me. I prefer a chilled glass of Chardonnay.

In the military, we are taught resiliency and looking out for your brother or sister-in-arms. Resiliency teaches the modern war-fighter surface level coping skills to overcome their obstacle in life so that they won't inadvertently become the weakest link in critical times of warfare, or worse yet, harm themselves. Not every veteran has been to the battlefield nor burdens the scars of war. I want to share with you my story of emotional resiliency and how I re-discovered myself post-divorce.

Emotional scars can be the most difficult to detect in someone unless they let their guard down and reveal their past pain. Only the compassionate heart can see agony that is manifested through trauma, rape, assault, disease, abuse, and any other life experience. Once you are tuned into emotion, you will see hurt in various stages all around you in nearly everyone you meet. They all, we all, have a story to tell. Never think for a moment that your life experience is void of assisting someone else through their past pain. Life is about the journey, not the destination. You could be that singular instrument of vitality that is absent in another life. My story goes something like this:

I had the unique life pleasure growing up in a little town you've never heard of known as Hershey, Nebraska. It was the all too familiar American upbringing with a blended parent household. I had chores, fought with my brother, had a stressed-out cat named Noah, hated my stepfather's comments, detested rules that applied only to me and not my big brother, and lived the small-town existence. My parents had split when I was a baby and my mother later remarried. My father wasn't really in the picture for the first several years and I know that affected me later in life. But whose childhood was perfect? If we can pinpoint something to complain about, we'll usually find it. From a very young age, I knew I had the Star-Spangled heart of an American Patriot. My stepfather was a Vietnam era veteran and my brother had enlisted in the Army and I knew without a doubt, I wanted to serve my country as well.

I enlisted in the U.S. Air Force in September 1997, as a personnelist, 3S0X1 (AFSC). Many military members carry this notion that their recruiter lied to them and are to blame for their military career misfortunes. Not me. I knew exactly what I was getting in to. With Google not yet around, information was still out there, and I went into active duty pretty informed. After graduating Basic Military Training, my technical school training and first duty station was Keesler AFB, Biloxi, Mississippi. Outside of training and the workplace battle rhythm, I had a fabulous time living the life of a free, independent, sometimes overly confident, single woman.

That part in the intro about no regrets? Yea...two thumbs back at this girl...loved it. In 2001, I was ready to venture on to another base and continue chasing life by the coat tails. I volunteered to accept a one-year assignment to Osan Air Base, South Korea, in exchange for the choice of my follow-on assignment. Personnelists were at any Air Force base around the world, so my options were infinite.

September 11, 2001, I landed in Korea unaware what tragedies were taking place in New York City. The military and life as I knew it, seemingly transformed overnight. At 21, I suddenly found myself in unfamiliar life territory without my friends, family, or good 'ole America.

I soon noticed a tall, handsome fella whom we shall refer to as Wilbur. One day while jamming Led Zeppelin in my dorm room, he stopped by and we seemed to mesh well. Before too long, hormones got the best of our wildfire close friendship, and well...you know the rest of the story. Anyway, one week my period decided not to show up as scheduled. Something we always look forward to, right girls? I bought a pregnancy test. Yep. Pregnant. Now what?

My mind was flooding with a million thoughts all at once. Abortion? Ugh, no. What if my traditional values family finds out I got pregnant before I got married? Should I get married to this guy I barely know? I would hate for my child to grow up like I did barely knowing their father. What if he moves to another base and my child never sees their father? My gut told me not to, but I couldn't bear to face my family. I was young and felt trapped that I had no choice, but to do the right thing.

While riding to the Korean consulate to get married, I had a sick feeling in my stomach. What the Hello Kitty was I doing?

Our follow-on base ended up being McChord AFB, Washington. Married life was an adjustment to say the least. We were both young, still navigating our young adulthood and being newbie parents. I won't lie; it was a difficult transition from an early 20's happy-go lucky life, to motherhood. We had a beautiful daughter named Sway Alexis, with the most genuine smile and carefree demeanor you've ever seen in a baby. 17 months later, another amazing daughter, Kaylee Alexandria became part of our little family.

Like most marriages, we had our battles, but nothing that we couldn't seemingly overcome. But, I began to notice Wilbur changing. Albeit, not for the better. Emotionally, he became frigid and warmed up only on his terms.

Let me paint you a picture of almost daily routine. Imagine, if you can, being home and your spouse walking through the door disregarding your loving greeting, avoiding conversation unless it were to his benefit, condescending attitude, or flat out ignoring you. Well let's just say, ignored until Mr. Man's personal bedroom needs required attention and miraculously his mood changed. The red flags could have blotted out the sun, but I was determined to make things work. If your relationship has more downs than ups, something is out of balance.

I always told that man he would make an astute lawyer in the way he could manipulate people with emotion, guilt, and pity. I fell for it time and time again. I felt like Porky Pig constantly taking pies in the face from the crowd favorite, Bugs Bunny. I knew I could be a great wife and that's all I wanted to be if given the chance. But it goes both ways and I felt like a doormat. Who wants to bust noses and beat down your spouse all the time in a marriage? Not me! That crap gets old and it's counterproductive to good order and household harmony.

If that weren't enough, I soon discovered he was cheating. He admitted it to me one day and I was stunned. What kind of Mickey Mouse Clubhouse shit was this? I didn't deserve this! What woman does, unless they are a capital B and holding out on their marital duties. I didn't get it. I took care of his needs, even when I felt he wasn't deserving of it. Because withholding from your spouse only generates more dissention. Then it happened again. And, again. And, again. And...again. Every time, Wilbur would display seemingly genuine guilt, apologize through waves of tears, and then do it all over again. Insert the definition of insanity right about now.

Ironically, he was an excellent father, but somehow skipped class on how to be an honorable husband. If sneaking around in the shadows wasn't enough, his emotional behavior towards me wasn't mending my heartstrings. I began to despise him. He was raised in a Christian home as well and somehow was able to justify his behavior towards me with his hand laying on the good book.

Disregarding his track record between the sheets, we were determined to make a new start and agreed to seek our physical needs only in each other. What a whirlwind. As you can guess, I committed and he, well...continued to seek out friends with benefits. We continued our façade to the outside world, maintaining composure all for the sake of toughing it out and hoping that the storms would eventually pass. They didn't.

My first sergeant began to notice my unhappiness as it began to seethe through my emotion at work. I was morphing into someone else. I became more numb by the day in that relationship. My Air Force family became my shoulder of support. Fellow female Airmen became my soundboard and helped me process the seemingly insurmountable feelings and hurt when I decided to share.

At this point, you're probably thinking: why didn't you

just leave Nickelette? Well, when there are kids in the equation, it's different. There would be spurts of good days and weeks that would mess with my head. Then, we'd go back to our normal. For instance, I'd say, maybe we are still adjusting and going through a rough patch? Or, maybe he's on his comma...you know, the male equivalent of being on your period.

Eventually, those feelings inevitably turned into: why the hell am I still here? Then, as you're daydreaming of what your life would have been like had you made different decisions, suddenly that Starbucks coffee scorches your tongue, or the whiff of a stinky baby diaper snaps you back into reality and you deal with it. The sick cycle of sharing a roof with someone displaying all the undiagnosed signs of Narcissistic Personality Disorder. You begin to question your own sanity as people like that can be so convincing and manipulating. It's so hard to describe unless you've been there. Yep, I got the sunburn and the t-shirt, but never an STD.

Just when things were almost palatable in Washington, I received a gut punch from my blind spot. Wilbur had volunteered for orders to Ramstein Air Base, Germany, without first conversing with me. Seriously, who does that?

My girlfriends and Air Force co-workers were pleading with me to seek life beyond my marriage, but I didn't want to break up my little family no matter how imperfect it was. I was not a quitter, never had been one. Or maybe I was becoming delusional; it was all blurry in those days. I made these decisions in life and, by God, I was going to own them.

We moved to Germany in 2006. Again, I found myself in a foreign land with no immediate support network, just Wilbur. Despite my positive outlook that a move might help us turn the wrinkled page in our marriage, it only compounded the problem. I began to lose my self-identity. Work was monotonous, kids were toddlers, and my husband seemed to be constantly going TDY in his job.

Often, I wouldn't discover he was leaving until the night before when he started packing his bags. As you can imagine, this communication and delivery style with most rational spouses would be unacceptable. No notice, work and childcare arrangements needed to be made, especially with toddlers in the picture.

Thankfully, I had understanding supervisors. The abnormal became the normal. Then, I began to appreciate his absence. As I settled into German culture, it suited my daughters and me.

Our relationship continued to deteriorate. One night, after yet another argument, he became physical and slammed me into a wall. I had a nasty trauma egg on my head and bruises on my arms. I had just become the victim of domestic abuse. He then had locked himself into the bedroom with the girls. As a mother, you can only imagine the thoughts going through my head. Is he about to do something dangerous to hurt my kids? Himself? He eventually cooled down and a friend took me to the hospital.

For the first time in my marriage, I was genuinely terrified of my husband. He had gone too far, and his anger boiled past acceptability. I informed my First

Sergeant and initiated a restraining order against Wilbur after that night.

We separated for a year and ventured opposite ways. I began to heal, make new friends, and slowly became my happy self once again. Our girls largely resided with me due to their father's work schedule and spent time with him on various weekends. Wilbur appeared to mature over the course of that year as well to the point that we were at least hospitable, once again, to each other.

You're probably saying that I gave him too many chances for redemption and you'd be right. I was approaching ten years of active duty service by that time and at a crossroads in my career. Pursuing a college degree in psychology was at the forefront of my personal goals as well as entertaining the possibility of giving my marriage one last ditch effort.

I'm a reasonable person to believe that people do have the ability to change...well, some people. It's a fault for some, strength for others. To still pursue my eventual retirement, I was ready to exit active duty and join the Air Force Reserve. We soon relocated to Travis AFB, California in 2009 to once again turn a different page in our relationship. Things were okay for a while with Napa Valley, San Francisco, Lake Tahoe, and the Redwoods within arm's reach.

Unfortunately, on the home front, it would be short lived and with our track record, I should have known better. It wasn't too many weeks before Wilbur was back to his usual self. Now that I was no longer working, he became overbearing and controlling with the family finances, even the pot of savings that I had from Germany became his money. I had to get permission to purchase a coffee. The car stereo had to always have Christian music playing; otherwise I would be chastised for my sinful ways. One day, I came home to find all my personal music albums and past life souvenirs in the dumpster as he felt he would take it upon himself to help cleanse my heart and vector me towards God. As if I couldn't find my own way. No one knew my pain or the level of emotional defeat I dealt with on a regular basis. I was feeling helpless by the day. Only now, I had no job, no family within 1,700 miles, no money to call my own, and I had no one to blame for stepping back into this circus marriage, but myself.

The slippery slide of lost identity turned into infinity; becoming more apparent every day.

We argued constantly, and the girls would frequently become scared of his unnecessary outbursts. We were like water and oil. No matter how much you shook the container, it was impossible to blend.

A car that I had originally purchased in Germany became his personal property and just before he deployed, he relocated the vehicle to his home state so that I would not have access to it during his absence. Magically, my name disappeared off of the title and I would never have the pleasure of driving it again. Even his father was speechless.

On his deployment, he decided he would notify our daughters via phone that we were divorcing; which was an unforgettable moment in their life, I assure you. A few weeks before his arrival back in the states, I was opening the mail and saw an envelope for Disney Cruises.

Honestly, nothing surprised me at that point. Inside, there were four tickets and another woman's name was in my place with the price of the cruise charged to our joint account. My stories of entertaining marital bliss in Toon Town could continue for hours, but that's not the point of this chapter of my life.

Now, you may be feeling various levels of emotion right now with the past few paragraphs. But I insist you refill your wine glass and wait patiently for the lessons of my life experience.

You see, life has a way of working itself through situations...either positively or negatively. You won't know until you're on the other side. I have come to know that karma indeed exists in this world and if you have a habit of planting seeds of thistle into your garden, those thorns have a way of finding you when you're not expecting.

Long story short, Wilbur moved out and I initiated divorce to the benefit of our small family. I had enough hurt to last a lifetime and it was visible that he had no intentions of ever apologizing.

To this day hearing his side in conversation, I will forever be the one to blame for his various actions while we were joined at the hip. I know it baffles me as well. The ludicrous whoopee cushion we referred to as marriage, finally deflated.

Let's all agree that we are responsible for our own actions in relationships.

Anyway, I decided that not having a man in my life

wouldn't be the worst thing for a while. I needed to rebuild my self-esteem once again, find true north, and re-discover happiness. I gained employment with the Air Force Reserve on active duty orders, finished my Bachelor's in psychology, started my Master's in human resources, and created a stable home life for my daughters.

All too often, people fall out of relationships and don't take the proper time, for them, to heal before plunging back into the dating scene. This inherently can perpetuate past relationship pitfalls and drown the next one before it has a chance to blossom. After all, its human nature to be desired, loved, and respected. Right? You bet.

Let's talk emotional recovery and resiliency. Everyone is wired differently, and we don't all respond to the same stimulus. Too often in the military and in life, we fall into bad relationships for the wrong reasons and often can't see the exit for our own pride and determination. I'm not saying that my divorce was a cakewalk. In fact, it was torture on my health, finances, and emotional well-being. But, it was necessary. It was ten years of open wounds that would only be healed with time.

Sometimes people need to be saved from themselves. This is where those of emotional stability and life experience become most important in mentoring your life. After the hurt dissipated, I found it particularly relieving to forgive. Not for his sake, but my own.

Poisonous emotion bound with stress, hatred, distrust, jealousy, and fear only serve to destroy the body's immunity and shorten lifespans. Trust me, let it go. In the silence of your thoughts, you will indeed discover clarity, resiliency, strength, courage, and determination to rise above the wreckage. Those moments define not only who you are, but who you're destined to be; possibly, in someone else's life down the road.

In 2013, I re-discovered love on a random Thursday with a man who knew my struggle in his own previous marriage. Love at first sight? Pfft...was what I used to say. Then it happened to me. Love was infused, restored, and continues to be a positive energy in our relationship and example for our four daughters.

Never underestimate the power of your relationship as you parade in front of your children. There aren't many gentlemen left out there and I lucked out, or maybe it was just my turn.

When a house is built, every board has a name and there's a predetermined purpose for load bearing, structural integrity, and supporting the roof from collapsing. Equally true is the structure of a relationship. It must be built on love, trust, vulnerability, healthy boundaries and dare I say emotional maturity.

Ole' man Hunter respects me, gives me space when I need it, supports my emotion, and accepts me for who I am. Out of mutual agreement, we don't share bank accounts, either. Bottom line, he gets me, and I understand him. You can't put a dollar figure on that level of genuine reciprocation.

A smile comes to my face when he leaves for work at 5 AM on his Harley, throttle wound leaving the driveway, and those obnoxious Thunderheader pipes aren't making us any more friends in the neighborhood. Love that man unconditionally. Someday, we hope to write a book on the importance of emotional intelligence and maturity in relationships. We married in June 2017, on the beach.

You remember Sway, my surprise baby? She's now in high school, learning to drive, and has plans to become a veterinarian. Kaylee will be in high school next year and has goals of someday becoming a fashion designer; she's business-minded for sure. As for my twin step-daughters, Salena loves animals and understands music as a second language, even going as far as to compose her own music. Lydia enjoys science, cooking, and has aspirations of becoming an Air Force Chaplain. Our 22-pound cat, Stormy, plays out his entitlement role by expecting ice water and refried beans as a treat. Don't ask how my husband discovered that. Cali, our other cat, is shy and could care less about cuddling with anyone, except Sway.

I later reconnected with my Dad and stepmom and bought back some precious time over the years. I love hanging out with my siblings when we get the chance. Ironically, I have a great relationship with my stepdad and relate to him on levels I never thought I would. My mother has been there for me through it all and I'll never forget her praying with me over the phone and helping get through another tough week.

It's my life and I wouldn't change it for anything. Oh yea, I almost forgot...I now drive my dream car with just my name on the title. After all, I'm the one making the payments.

That part about no regrets? It's true. They're just life lessons moving forward.

Life and its lessons happen in irreplaceable moments. Exist in those moments. Learn from them. Be there for one another... navigate life together. It'll be over before you know it.

Peace, Wine, and Love...Nic

PEGGY ZUBER, SFC
US NAVY AND US ARMY

My life as a Sailor, Soldier, and a Defense Contractor

I come from a military family. My dad, Ray Zuber, was a retired Navy Chief who survived the attack on Pearl Harbor and went to Gitmo, Cuba several times. My mom worked for the Navy out processing center in Long Beach, California. At a young age I had the opportunity to go to France, England, Haiti, Puerto Rico, St. Thomas and various parts of Mexico which inspired me to travel. I joined the US Navy, went to Basic in Orlando, Florida and then my first duty station was Roosevelt Roads, Puerto Rico where I was assigned to Atlantic Fleet Weapons Training Facility in the Electronic Warfare department. We had a few incidents in Puerto Rico where folks would shoot into the base near a certain road.

I thought I had wanted to be a Communication Tech, so I visited Sabana Seca. My department wanted me to go to Electronic Warfare School, but I decided I wanted to be a Radioman instead. I transferred to the Communication Center to learn the Rate of Radioman OJT and put in for Radioman "A" School. I was accepted into Radioman "A" school in San Diego, California. The school wanted to me to stay and teach classes, but I wanted to do some traveling. I was assigned to Alameda Air Station, near San Francisco, where I worked as a Radioman. During this time there were a lot of bomb threats and we had to have Marine guards accompany us when we delivered messages to the ships in port. Also, I had volunteered to be a part of an exercise at Moffet Field, Mountain View, California.

I completed my active duty Navy commitment and joined the US Army Reserves, Military Intelligence Company as a 05C, where I was a Communication Ratt Rig Operator. Soon after I got out of the Navy, I heard that one of the Senior Chief Radioman back in Alameda was arrested for espionage. He was a part of the Walker Spy Ring. That just floored me, how could anyone do such a thing?

With the Army Reserves, I was able to go to Darmstadt, Germany for a few weeks. Then I moved back home to Tulsa, after living a year in Holland. I joined 486 Civil Affairs Unit Broken Arrow, OK and had the opportunity work REFORGER in Belgium for several years.

I requested to go for training as a 92Y and then on to Instructor School. I transferred to 95th USAR TNG Des Moines, Iowa where I trained solders 92Y Military Occupation Unit Supply Specialist.

I served 21 good years and retired as an SFC United States Army.

After 9/11 happened, I went to work in Iraq supporting the military as a Field Buyer for KBR living and working out of a tent. We went through training and in processing in Houston, TX. It was KBR's first large group to go to Iraq. We went through medical first and then went through different training classes. Nothing was written down. You had to be in the lobby of the hotel and listen to see when the next training class was. At midnight, I went and got my ID made. We left for the airport at a very early hour. We then arrived in Kuwait and boarded busses to Iraq. We worked 12 hours a day, 7 days a week. Kuwait was so hot; I thought my brain was boiling in the month of July.

My assignment was a Field Buyer for supplies and

services for base operation in Kuwait and Iraq.

When you left your tent at night, you had a flashlight to find your way out of your tent. You had enough time to shower and then inspect your sleeping bag for any "visitors" and get your mosquito net arranged. You were lulled to sleep by the sound of generators running and black hawks flying. They were so loud they sounded like they were landing on your tent. Then usually around 1 AM the incoming shells would begin. They would come in threes, so if it was close you would run to the bunker, if not then you would continue sleeping.

Once I had received a care package from a friend with homemade salsa and bag of chips. My teammates got some plastic bowls and plates and then said we are going to have a salsa party in our tent #8. Then the incoming started so we grabbed our vest and helmets and sat back down to eat.

The incoming wasn't that close, besides if we left the food something would get in it and if we took it with us something would get in it. Sometimes a group of us would go to the Enlisted Club and act like we were going out on the town.

At the EM club we would eat microwave pizza, and something called Near Beer, it was non-alcoholic. Daily and nightly we had to take cover in the bunker with the incoming Rocket Propelled Grenades (RPG) fired into the base.

I started working at the Air Station Balad and they were needing help in Tikit, so I flew there on a Chinook. This was before Saddam Hussein was found. My boss wanted us to leave the base and solicit vendors. I explained that was very dangerous. Their response: "It takes too long to inspect everyone." The camp manager agreed something would happen one day. It was then time for my rest and relaxation rotation, but I had no way to leave because all of the aircraft had been grounded due to the attacks.

At that time there were no American convoys traveling, just Third World Nationals. I had an American vendor who came to Tikit, who was acting as Canadian, take me to Anaconda so I could catch a flight out. The convoy had been cancelled, so he said it was up to me to travel with them or wait for another time. I took the opportunity and when I got to Anaconda, they were not letting civilians fly out so I took a convoy out to Kuwait.

The convoy had one military gunner in front and one military gunner in back and probably ten tanker trucks in between. While traveling, a sand storm came up and part of the trucks made a wrong turn. We were at the beginning of the convoy, so we waited for the rest of the convoy to come back. In the meantime, the gunner took off. It wasn't long before the rest of the convoy got back with us and the gunner was about a mile down the road from us. Our truck side mirror was hit with a big rock and the truck in front of us had a window hit with rocks.

We arrived at one base and got fuel but had to spend the night because we couldn't travel at night. The next morning, I arrived at a base right at the border of Iraq and Kuwait. That was as far as the convoy went, and they would now travel back up north. I then caught another convoy and headed into Kuwait.

I received an offer from Parsons Corporation to be a

Senior Buyer and Subcontract Administrator with better rotation. I was assigned to Palestine Hotel and then on to Kirkuk. The insurgents blew up the Kirkuk Ceyhan Oil pipeline monthly. Then after an RFP attack on the base, it was called all clear.

Everyone went back to their living quarters and then BOOM, BOOM, BOOM! Incoming had started and caught the ammunition dump on fire. I was lying face down and the military came by and said, "Run to the DFAC! Run or die!"

We went to the DFAC and got into the bunkers. The firing lasted for a good hour and a half. I'm glad we left our compound, or someone could have been hurt really bad.

The next day I had went out of the company's compound. When I came back, the gates were shut. Explosives had been found right by our living quarters. The CIA discovered it had been the welder and his son who had been working in our compound. I asked to transfer to Amman, Jordan. There we had to be aware of our surroundings in case an event took place.

Once we were sitting in the Intercontinental Hotel and in came the Interim Prime Minister of Iraq. He was only a few feet from us and waved at us. The security guards were everywhere. That was so awesome, and then we thought maybe we better leave the area, because we didn't know if there would be some terrorist activity.

During our work there, there were some hotel attacks and once we had to relocate and work out of another building. I worked there for a year and then on to Huntsville, Alabama supporting various projects for the reconstruction of Iraq.

For security at the Palestine Hotel, there were Gurkha's from Nepal and Armor Group from the UK. I now work for Cherokee Nation Businesses supporting governing contracts as a Contracts Analyst II. I am proud to be a US Citizen and looking for other Overseas Opportunities supporting the US Military.

RITA MILLER, COLONEL
UNITED STATES AIR FORCE

Breaking the Infamous Glass Ceiling

The Beginning

"Hello, Mom; are you there?" Silence. I was at the phone booth outside my dorm at Lackland AFB, Texas, on a blustery, cold afternoon. It was February 1984, and I was using my allotted time to call family and let them know we had arrived safely at Basic Training. I was telling Mom I had joined the Air Force and that I would be gone for the next twenty weeks for training. Silence. Then she finally said, "We will talk then. I love you." I replied with a teary, "I love you and dad, too." I was 24 years old and had my Bachelor's Degree. Not being able to find a job in education, I needed to secure an income. I had always wanted to join the Air Force and now I could...on my own.

That first morning, sleeping soundly in my twin bed, reveille came over the speaker, into our luxurious, forty-eight-bed dorm room! "Oh, what have I gotten myself into?" was the first thing I thought. Trying to get showered, dressed, and out to formation was not easy with forty-eight females thinking they were home and didn't have to hurry. That attitude changed and we all adjusted quickly.

I was selected as a flight leader with twelve of my fellow dorm mates, which challenged me to the full extent--especially when we returned from physical training one hot afternoon and our flight of twelve beds and the contents of our lockers were strewn all over the place.

I was called to report in to the Master Sergeant who was standing amidst the mess. Nose to nose with me, using profanity and emanating bad breath, he proceeded to tell me what a lousy leader I was and how I was ever placed in a leadership position was beyond him. He turned and left. I took a minute to process what had just happened. Then, as if that wasn't enough, our Technical Instructor gave me the news that my flight would not be going on liberty the coming weekend to downtown San Antonio. Also, we would be moving all forty-eight beds, cleaning and waxing the floors, cleaning all grout in the bathroom, putting the beds back, then making all forty-eight of them according to regulation. I was about to explode!

I took some breaths, assembled my flight, and gave orders. Complaining was what I heard first; then they heard me! We didn't have time to complain: we needed to jump in as a team and do what we had been directed to do...and we would, I relayed to them in a very stern voice. That dorm room and showers looked like new when we got finished, then everyone returned, very surprised at how nice it looked.

Fast forward to last day of our academics...guess who got the most improved, teamwork award...yes, our flight! I began to feel like I was being singled out to see if I would come unglued.

The next test was on our day to practice the graduation march. I was called to the TI and informed that he and the other TI's didn't like how my blue cap sat on my head...they were taking me out of the march. At first, I was thinking I wasn't graduating, but they assured me I was. They just didn't like the way my hat sat on my head. Yes, I was upset since I wanted to march in formation during graduation. Instead, I was assigned to cut the grass along the concrete curb with a hand cutter...yikes!

Once again, I didn't let my feelings of anger and disgust show, since I was sure that was what they were wanting. I became a human edger and did as asked. Once again, I got a compliment on doing a great job of edging. The final day came to leave this hell. I graduated with two stripes due to having my degree. I was put on a plane and flown to my next destination...Technical Training!

The plane landed at Denver International Airport and all of us heading for the next class were loaded on a bus. Next stop...Lowry Air Force Base, Colorado. My first thought was that it was beautiful there, with the Rocky Mountains standing tall and majestic.

After processing in, we were shown to our rooms; I would share mine with ONE other airman. All that was on my mind was to make it through these thirteen weeks and go home. I didn't want to be put in a leadership position or stand out in any way. Get through the Munitions Armament Specialist training and go home. So, do you think that happened?

The third day, I received a notification to show at the parade pad for marching instruction. Marching instruction? Was I going to march in a band? I didn't even play an instrument! I showed up as instructed and was immediately handed a yellow rope to wear over my shoulder. I would wear this anytime I had the uniform on as a FLIGHT LEADER!!!!! What? No...no...no! What was I doing that made me look like a leader or that I even had the potential to lead?

The awful thoughts of Basic Training came flowing back to me. I wanted to let them know I was not interested, but that would have placed a noose around my neck.

I made it through Tech School. I was second in my class. I had been first, until I got news that my grandmother had succumbed to pancreatic cancer; this caused me to be unable to concentrate on an upcoming test, which I failed. I was allowed to retake it and did much better. Again, I was just glad to have it all behind me. I had three weeks left after returning from her funeral; I was ready to be home and just build bombs. After all, that is what I had trained to do.

Returning to Tulsa, Oklahoma, June 1985, to the 138th Tactical Fighter Group, was one of the happiest days in a long time. I was even happier when I got a position in an elementary school teaching fifth grade that fall. Everything seemed to be falling into place and I looked back with pride on what I had done. I had signed the papers, committing to six years with the Air National Guard in Tulsa. I could do that. I would walk away proud of serving my country.

I suppose God saw how I loved what I did and gave that view to my superiors, too. I was "highly encouraged" after three years to apply for officer school. I said I was happy being enlisted; then I thought about it and how I would be able to lead and make a difference in my own unit.

Before I knew it, I was on my way to McGhee Tyson Air National Guard Base in Tennessee to attend the Academy of Military Science. I would be there for six weeks. I managed to make it to the fifth week before I was made "Squadron Commander" of all the cadets!

I actually enjoyed the time at AMS--even the short stint of leadership. The only traumatizing event that happened to me was hell night, held on the fourth night there, I later learned. I had just gotten off duty as Officer of the Day, then gone to my room to change into my gym clothes. I had just hung up my uniform when there was a knock at the door and it flew wide open, with our female TI shouting, "Fire! Fire! Get out now!" I said, "Yes Ma'am, I just need to get dressed." I only had my bra and panties on. She yelled "You have no time, get out NOW!" I thought, I am not going out there in just this, looked over at my bed and jerked the bedspread off, tied it around me, and ran out to formation.

Thank goodness everyone had to have eyes forward, but I still heard snickering. All the TI's were telling us how terrible we were; that they didn't know how we had ever been selected to be an officer. We were lower than low. After a few minutes of this belittling, little did I know it was going to get worse.

They did a left turn, preparing us to march to the gym. The gym? Really? What could that mean? As we started to march, I didn't realize that the guy behind me was on my bedspread. The spread pulled me backward, and I let out a scream. "HALT!" The TI came back to where we were, looked at me and replied, "Do you have a problem, cadet?" I quickly came back with a "No sir!" to which he smirked and shook his head.

We marched to the gym without any other incidents. Once there, hell began! We had to run around the gym until we were told to stop. Now in a makeshift toga it was not an easy feat, but I accomplished all the sit-ups and pushups, along with ridiculous questions, without once losing my bedspread toga!

It would have been less of a stressful event if I could have gotten my gym clothes on! Five weeks later, I pinned on my gold bars, signifying Second Lieutenant. I was ready for the next chapter.

Before leaving for AMS, my commander had placed me in charge of Aircraft Maintenance Squadron, effective upon my return. When I got back, I learned my first hard lesson of the "good old boys" games and became the pawn.

Integrity first was not always upheld, I noted. I was assigned as the Administrative Officer because, as I was told by that same commander, "Women belong behind typewriters anyway." I was in shock that he had the nerve to say that, but it was only the beginning of what would be many remarks against females in the military. Besides, he was a colonel, so I guessed he could say those remarks.

The Middle

I remained in that position for about four years. I was promoted to First Lieutenant while in that role. Finally, making Captain, I was placed in the traditional (weekend) officer position over Maintenance Operations Flight. They were a great team of people and made my job easy. My chief was the same chief I had in munitions! It was nice to have him on my side. He looked out for the best opportunities for me. Chief Johnson was, and still is, a sounding board when I need one.

Following my stint in MOF, I was offered a full-time position with Aircraft Maintenance Squadron. Yes, the one I had originally been assigned to before leaving for officer's school! I was more than happy to take this position. The bittersweet part was leaving my teaching post. Still, I felt I could make a difference with the airmen as I had done with the young people I had taught. I would learn that being the only female commander within the group would bring to light the gender biases and harassment existing both within and outside of the group. This just gave me a challenge—not an obstacle.

Being one of the only three females in munitions had made me tough and taught me how to handle the inequality.

I loved being the Aircraft Maintenance Officer. I learned that, as an officer leading such a diverse group of thinkers, both young and old, would prove to be a challenge. One I accepted with a vengeance. Perhaps I could change the old way of thinking, bringing more gender equality into the mix. Only my commanders and officers over me never changed, and disappointment left me feeling defeated most of the time.

I was frequently not included in meetings where my squadron was discussed, but later told what my squadron would do. I was infuriated. I was ordered (forced) to hire or promote "friends" into positions within my squadron that didn't meet the qualifications, and vice versa for the ones I had put forward for promotions who never seemed to get them.

When I would voice my concerns or let them know I didn't agree, I would hear, "Oh it must be that time of the month!!!!" I would have filed complaints on them, but it was like I was working with the mafia. My career would be over, and they would see to it.

These are the same commanders that stated about a woman, "It was a waste of good breasts" when it was found out that she was a lesbian.

I began losing all trust for my leaders at this time and was wondering if I had made the right decision to be around this on a daily basis. Making me even sicker to my stomach, this particular commander weaseled his way to General!!! Disgusting! Good old boy politics.

To my surprise, I was moved to the finance position three years later, at another tech school, and into a group that had not had a leader for several years. I came in right after September 11, 2001, to a group of people including me that had not been through a war time. We learned so much together and became a close group despite our differences. I had the pleasure of going through the largest travel audit by Air Force Audit Agency (AFAA) on a guard unit. I was proud of the hard work and dedication of this small group. While in this position, I was promoted to Lieutenant Colonel, and would serve as the Wing Comptroller for six years.

Under a new commander, I was back in Maintenance in 2007 in the full-time maintenance officer position in maintenance squadron since the Commander was a traditional. With this move, I had now been over every section in the Maintenance Group but the Deputy and Group Commander. I was moved back over to the Aircraft Maintenance Squadron after three years and was under the command of three different pilots who needed to be in a command position to make Colonel.

Between the Maintenance officers and Maintenance Chiefs (and some very dedicated technicians), we educated them about their Maintenance Group and their jobs.

During my tenure there, we deployed to Iraq for Operation Iraqi Freedom in 2007 and 2008. We had people lent out to other units in support of those operations and others. It was crazy! I was deployed with the group as the Maintenance Officer in 2008 and once again in 2011 for Operation Iraqi Dawn, which would be the closing down of the war on Iraq.

We were the last fighter unit deployed to Iraq to get the troops safely to base and headed home. It was a very gratifying deployment to know we had played a part in helping the US troops to go home.

Once we arrived home, I was informed my paperwork for promotion to Colonel had been approved. At first, I thought it had been a mistake. I even verified with my commander and Wing Commander. They assured me it was not a mistake. First, though, my commander had to leave. He wasn't ready, so he stayed in that position until September 2012, nearly a year after I had been approved.

I was promoted to rank of Colonel and would be the first female Group Commander of the 138th Maintenance Group. I was also the first person to be fully trained in maintenance and take command in over 30 years!

I had achieved what I thought would never happen because of all the prior actions and backward thinking of my previous leaders. I persevered. Not without enduring doubt from others. Not without gender biases and discrimination, which were dealt out with no remorse. Not without heartbreak and loss. I will say that as I endured the negative, it was educating me on what a leader IS NOT!

I remained Commander in Maintenance until December 2014, at which time the new Wing Commander had a pilot to promote, of course, placing him in my position. I was moved over to command the Mission Support Group. Again, I was among a wonderful group of talented and dedicated airmen.

On to The Next Chapter...

I retired in December 2015; in attendance at the ceremony were family, friends, and those in whose lives I had made a difference while serving as their commander. I had enjoyed the travel to the sites of Volk Field, Wisconsin, and Gulfport Training Center--just to stay in those fashionable Chemical Suits-- Wittering AB, England; Ramstein AB, Germany; Incirlik AB, Turkey; and to some very exotic deployments to work with the Japanese Navy in Kauai, Hawaii. It wasn't an easy thirty-one years, but it taught me, brought me, and grew me to where I am today. I endured more than will ever been known: much is better left unsaid. I left knowing that I had broken through that infamous "glass ceiling" that was constantly above the head of every female on base.

Discrimination is still alive on base. My hope is that I was a role model for those females who aspire to do great things, both for themselves and others! I retired with my head held high--my integrity intact--knowing I put others before myself and ensuring excellence in all I did.

ROSIE RICHARDS, CAPTAIN
UNITED STATES ARMY

Anecdotes and Observations: Women in the Military

I have no doubt in my mind that the United States Army drastically improved my life in many ways. The Army was the best fit for me; my personality, my professional ambitions, my enthusiasm to see the world, and my sense of duty. I slowly learned, years into my Army career, of the commitment and sacrifice, moral and ethical quandaries, bureaucratic impasses, and the leadership rollercoaster that military members face on a daily basis. I could not predict where my career would take me.

I struggled to put pen to paper when writing about my personal journey as a woman in the Army. On one hand, I feel my experience, moments ranging from professional satisfaction to absolute anguish, are felt at all levels of the military by all people. After some reflection, I began extracting some observations, themes, and life lessons I feel are unique to being a woman in the military. The following anecdotes explain why I joined and what I have learned from various Army scenarios, all of which I consider "Aha moments" in my career.

What is your *Civility Quotient?*

I have never been an obvious choice for the military, but public service has always been my calling. My first story dives into the moment I committed myself to pursuing a career in the Armed Forces, and to be honest, I came to this realization in an unlikely place.

After enjoying my college life in a small Oregon community, I moved to New York City to pursue a graduate degree in public administration. The majority of new students attended the first class on a rainy, Monday night, around 6pm. We filed into the 200-plus person lecture hall on the first floor of a building, located in the heart of NYC, excitedly brushing off the rain and finding our seats. The professor stood in front of the class, exuding charisma and knowledge. He started off by asking the group about our *civility quotient*. My mind raced. What the heck was a *civility quotient*? Instantly, I felt out of place. Does that even sound familiar? Did I learn this in college? My mind was blank. I had nothing. He followed up with another stumping question, "How many of you have heard of William Dawes?" A few hands went up. Ok. Great. Now I am definitely questioning my education (or at least retention) and my ability to recall data.

This is just the first class of a 2-year program, and I am already 0 for 2. The professor knew he had us. He then dove into the retelling of a story from the Revolutionary War, highlighted in Malcolm Gladwell's book, *Tipping Point*.

The professor was referring to the midnight ride of William Dawes and Paul Revere. I highly recommend the book, but for now, allow me to summarize. Both Revere and Dawes road out to alert the public of an imminent British attack, riding from Boston to Lexington and Concord, notifying small towns along the way. Revere, a "connector," had a broad social network allowing him to spread his message quickly and effectively. Community members trusted Revere. His *civility quotient* was high.

Dawes, who had less knowledge of the area, weaker community ties, and less effective communication skills, led to a weak showing of Patriots from the countryside along his route.

The professor circled the story back to the group of attentive students. Through this retelling, it appears that Revere leveraged his relationships, built on years of service, to accomplish an important mission for his community. Dawes, while still involved in his community, may not have had the connections leveraged by Revere, leading to fewer people answering his call for support. The *civility quotient* simply measures the level of involvement and trust you hold in the community. This prompted a list of reflective questions to the classroom of future public servants.

- What is your *civility quotient?*
- What will you focus on in your community?
- How much time will you commit to helping one another?
- What are your civic goals?
- How will you achieve these goals in your community?

I went through these questions, reflecting on my professional goals and interests. I wanted to give back to my family, my community, my Country. I wanted to see the world, be on a team, and make an impact. That led me to the first "Aha moment." I would join the United States Army.

<u>Welcome to the Army, Lieutenant</u>

"Everything you see or hear or experience in any way at all is specific to you. You create a universe by perceiving it, so everything in the universe you perceive is specific to you." - Douglas Adams, *Mostly Harmless.*

The phrase, "perception is reality" remains prevalent among the junior ranks in the Army. I always had a difficult time with this one. Maybe because I believe that reality is reality; that a person can be held accountable for their actions, not a perception of events. Perhaps that perspective is naïve, especially since I have so many examples of Army life where the perception of a soldier can make or break his or her career.

As a Second Lieutenant, I made the trip to my first duty station, Korea. My leadership sent me north, as the only officer for my company and battalion, to serve in Area I, managing a small group of soldiers, KATUSAs and Korean National personnel. My team and I drove an hour for company meetings in Area II, and six hours south to Area IV for battalion-wide functions. I enjoyed the independence of Area I. The team worked hard, determined to stand out as the best unit in the battalion. I dedicated that year to my team and my work. I believed in good communication with my commander and executive officer (XO), especially since I was so "far away from the flagpole," as some soldiers say, meaning we had little oversight on our day to day operations. This meant consistent phone calls and text messages at night, to notify the commander that personnel arrived home safely from our many late-night missions.

I felt as though I took the initiative, possibly putting my commander's mind at ease knowing he had a dedicated, thoughtful leader in Area I.

One week, during our company training meeting, my commander said that my NCO and I needed to visit battalion headquarters. This would be our first trip that far south. We were excited to meet the staff and leaders, including a meeting with the battalion commander. We were doing great work in Area I, so we were happy to load into a van at 0400 and make the trip to Area IV. Once in the van, everyone instantly put in headphones and slept to pass the time. Upon our arrival, the officers reported to the battalion commander's office. I noticed the battalion XO greet my commander quietly, then slipped, together, into the battalion commander's office and closed the door. While I sat alone in the waiting area, I slowly realized that, maybe, just maybe, I was not called down to Daegu for a congratulatory meeting with the leadership. Maybe it was something else, something wrong.

I racked my brain for possible issues with the Area I mission or my team's dynamic and work load. What could it be? I did not have a clue. Just then, my commander exited the office, slightly stooped, and moved to a nearby empty desk in the corner. The battalion XO signaled for me to follow her into the battalion commander's office. I stood at attention until invited to sit. Even though something felt off about this encounter, I was still so enthusiastic...so excited about meeting the Lieutenant Colonel.

I sat quietly, and the battalion commander began his introduction. "Welcome, do you know why I asked you here today?" he said.

"No, sir. I'm not sure why I'm here," I responded, smiling. "As an officer, I am required to investigate any accusations of wrong doing in the battalion. In your case, the wife of your commander alleged that you and your commander were having an affair."

I was completely shocked. Frozen in my seat. My mind raced. I did not know my commander that well, and I definitely did not flirt with him. He never visited me onsite, and I only saw him once a week for our meetings in Area II.

Some soldiers in the unit made comments about his dereliction of duty, apathy, poor leadership, but I honestly did not know him that well. How could his wife have this perception of me? To this day, I do not know what she looks like, her name, nothing. But there I was, in the hot seat, answering uncomfortable questions about my personal life, volunteering my phone for his inspection, and attempting to defend my honor and correct this misperception.

I did not have an inappropriate relationship with my commanding officer.

At this point, I felt lucky that I had saved my text messages (to the company commander) for the Battalion Commander to review. I always prefaced my messages with, "Sir," and discussed only work. I left the office feeling as though I made a strong case. I then wrote a summary of my interactions with my commander on a sworn statement, to include taking an oath, swearing that I had told the truth.

As a new (single) officer in the military, this was my introduction to the implicit bias attached to women in uniform. That single event changed my professional interactions in Korea and at future organizations. I developed a strategy to protect myself from being accused of adultery at all future duty stations. Initially, I became more guarded. I never texted or called my commander after 6pm again. I always had the NCOIC conduct the phone calls or send the "mission accomplished, everyone is home safe" text. I then made a point to introduce myself to the soldiers' spouses to limit their faulty assumptions about me. I felt like I was protecting myself from an invisible enemy, always on guard and ready to prove my innocence. This was my second "Aha moment."

Welcome to the Army, Lieutenant.

Manifestations of Bias

I reflected on this event many times in my career. Through these reflections, I found that the perception of destructive behavior unequally focuses on women in the military. This was my third "Aha moment." I believe this is related to working in a predominantly male profession. I started taking notes of bias or preconceptions soldiers made towards women in the unit. The following provides brief notes on my personal interactions that demonstrate prejudice towards women:

- My old company commander would joke with our newly married orderly soldier if she was pregnant yet on a daily basis. The soldier's NCO approached me after a week of harassment. She asked me to talk to the commander, stating that the soldier was uncomfortable with these jokes. As the platoon leader, I stepped in to tell my commander that behavior was inappropriate, to his astonishment. "I was only kidding!" he replied defensively, "I'll stop. I didn't think that was a big deal."

- A friend on staff returned from a mission planning conference, where he retold the story that the leaders of that organization bragged about holding their hail and farewell at a strip club.

- When I was on battalion staff, a new officer began in-processing to our unit. I was happy to see another woman in the officer ranks at our battalion. In less than a week, I overheard staff officers at work betting on whether she would sleep with an officer or a warrant officer first.

- While stationed in Germany, I went on a mission to provide staff support to a company conducting training with our NATO allies. I learned a lot from the mission and thought everything went fairly well. About a week later, I met with the company commander to get her thoughts on the mission. She mentioned that while drama was minimal, it still bubbled up during the 2-week mission.

Apparently one of the warrant officer's wives heard my voice in the background during his phone call home (while he stood in our operations cell). His wife called other wives to tell them that women (aside from his commander, who was also a woman) were on the mission. This spun up a few wives who called their husbands, worried about infidelity. This made it to the company commander's level (my roommate during the mission), who had to assure the families that no inappropriate behavior was taking place.

- While in the US, on Brigade staff, I worked with a Chief Warrant Officer 4. While leaving on a Friday evening after 1700, we passed a soldier coming into the building wearing personal gym attire. Chief said, "Ma'am, I have to tell you something. But once we get outside." I said, "Sure."

  He started, "Ma'am, did you see her? Did you see what she was wearing? I mean, you wonder why people start rumors or guys hit on you looking like that. I mean, it's like she's asking for it."

  I responded, "Chief, I totally disagree. She was wearing a baggy (high-collar) t-shirt with cutoff sleeves, spandex pants, and sneakers. She looked like a normal person going to the gym after work. She probably just got called back in from the gym. What are you talking about?"

  He replied, "First, she shouldn't wear that in the Brigade building. Second, I guess I'm old. I would never let my niece walk around like that, in clothes that are just asking for it."

  I answered back, "Chief, I have seen tons of men walk in and out of that building after hours in gym attire. That doesn't bother you. And what do you mean she's asking for it? She looked totally normal."

  This back and forth continued. The conversation ended with me explaining double standards and bias, but at that point, we were both exhausted and ready to go home.

Moving Forward

My friends and I often discussed our observations as women in the military. We found some commonalities in how we navigated through some uncertain situations. In some cases, we assimilate to our surroundings, acting guarded, walking in groups of three or more to limit gossip about an imaginary affair, or building relationships with your co-worker's spouse to assure you are not a threat.

We are protecting ourselves from that invisible enemy called prejudice. In other cases, women stand up for each other, stomping out the mean-spirited rumors that would inevitably weaken our teams. My friends have had so many experiences with fighting these biases. These conversations with one another helped me make sense of my experiences in the Army and encouraged me to learn more about my own prejudices, habits, and actions.

Early on in my career, I focused on studying doctrine, staying focused on professional priorities, and exceeding standards set by the military. I learned to remain professional and aware of my actions and the actions of others. As I mature as an officer, while I continue to maintain my studies and my professional focus, I now attempt to strengthen my relationships and reach out for mentorship.

Mentorship, while discussed at all levels of Army schools, can be difficult to come by on a personal level. While many organizations provide leader professional development programming, the one-on-one mentors are never automatic. My luck with this is mixed.

As a first lieutenant, I learned that you cannot force leaders, like Battalion Commanders (BCs), to be mentors. I received a great evaluation from my senior rater, the BC, when I was a first lieutenant. I went to the S1 to schedule my evaluation out-brief. The response was lackluster. The BC did not understand why I would want an out-brief after getting such a good evaluation. While I was looking for professional guidance, the BC provided some generalized notes and ended the meeting fairly quickly.

After that meeting, I began reaching outside of the organization for mentorship. I wrote to old commanders, instructors, and people I worked with in the past to get answers to questions regarding my professional development. As a Captain, I began work on Brigade staff under the Support Operations Officer (SPO). This was the first time in my career I worked for someone in the same building willing to provide me with regular feedback and mentorship. It was incredible, but short lived.

In this case, I learned that once you create the bond with your mentor, you can reach out regularly. No matter where they are in the world. And in the meantime, you can always read. Some of my best professional development came from books, ranging from titles on the Chief of Staff's reading list, to modern organizational leadership publications, to autobiographies. I just started *Lean In, Women, Work, and the Will to Lead* by Sheryl Sandberg. I look forward to learning a lot.

In the last 30 years, women made a lot of progress in the Armed Forces. I am grateful for my opportunity to serve with some incredible men and women. I love being a soldier. The anecdotes above are not a commentary on all men in the military. Not at all. I have met so many intelligent, thoughtful leaders, both men and women, during my time in the Army. For the service women reading this, I am sure these anecdotes sound familiar, definitely not surprising. For others, these stories simply provide you, the reader, with some perspective on what women face in their careers. Women have made a lot of progress in the military, but there is still more to be done.

SAVANNAH OTT, 1ST LT
UNITED STATES ARMY

Readers – I divided the following essay into two segments. The first piece I wrote after a particularly influential day at the office. The second is a response to my first piece. The following writing is not meant to be negative, but informative. Informative for those who may not have had these experiences, those who are still in training, or those who have had these experiences and may want to read about it from a different perspective. I ask that you read until the end... and enjoy!

Stereotypes, Perception and Speaking Up

Gender inequality is real. I can only speak from my current experiences in the Army, but I promise it is real. As I approach my fourth full year of active duty service, I continue to see examples of inequality throughout the ranks. I have a ten-year-old goddaughter who recently wrote a paper about stereotypes for her Girl Scout troop. Her mother, my aunt, suggested that her daughter ask me about stereotypes for women in the military. I struggled to translate my stories to a child's perspective and lessen the severe criticism I hold against the current stereotypes. In the following pages I will summarize my experiences with stereotypes and gender-specific treatment. But first, her (albeit short) essay:

Stereotypes: Women in the Military

From Savannah, my cousin who is in the military. Not everyone believes women should be in the military and many military men don't treat women as equals. Some men do not think that a woman can be as strong as a man, don't like to see a woman do the same job as them and do better, and they can be mean to women who can do a job well. Women are not as free to be themselves as men.

They are expected to be friendly and outgoing. If they are serious or harsh they may be called bad names but it's okay for a man to act that way. Men are expected to be strong leaders and act forceful. It is easier for men in the military because there are many more men in the military than women and they get along with each other more easily than they get along with women. There are more men leaders than women leaders. How to change this stereotype is that we need more women in the military. Right now, the Army is about 15% women and 85% men. Men often don't see or understand women's issues.

The above paragraph is generalized, and I am sure any doubter of gender inequality could read it and punch a lot of holes in this ten-year-old's argument. The following paragraphs are the facts and show exactly why this ten-year-old's argument is not far from the truth regarding the inequality women face in the US military.

Part I: Romania

There I was, on a nine-month trip to Eastern Europe, primarily as a "show-of-force" mission in response to Russia. I was part of a small 12-15 person element that provided logistical support to our helicopters and crews on the base.

This deployment was not like others in combat zones; often we had weekends free and the ability to go off-base and visit the local areas. Anyone in the military knows that these environments are ripe for fraternization and adultery. As one of the few females at that base and the only female officer, I was particularly careful about who I spent my spare time with. There were three other lieutenants (LTs), all male aviators. For clarity's sake, I'll tell you that I was engaged, two were married and one was gay. From my point of view, we were safe to hang out without fear of emotions or attraction getting into the mix. I also assumed we would be excused from the rumor mill.

Just like any deployment, over time tensions rise and friction is common. This usually has to do with being in such a close, constrained environment with the same people for such an extended amount of time. As young LTs we were under the microscope of our soldiers and our commanding officers 24/7. Our original group of four LTs drifted into three. The three of us took a weekend hiking trip to northern Romania and had a fantastic time. After that weekend, the aviation company commander pulled aside one of the LTs and told him that he needed to spend less time with our group of lieutenants and more time with his subordinates. He complied.

He spent more time with his soldiers and the other pilots. We would catch up occasionally, but we did not spend time outside of the work place together. Now, just a few months into the deployment, I was left with one peer to spend my time with. We had a lot in common - we were both in love with our significant others, we both planned to run a remote Marine Corps marathon held on base, neither of us drank, and we enjoyed talking about religion, politics, ethics, etc. We would work out together, go to the dining facility together, and overall spend most of our spare time together.

As you can guess, in such a close environment, his company commander had an issue with all of the time we spent together. With some major training exercises complete and only a couple of months until our handover with the incoming unit, his commander pulled him aside and told him that he should not spend time with me any longer due to "perception."

I will not throw stones at leadership decisions as I am sure that I have made many poor choices myself. I believe that with most actions that promote gender inequality, it is done unintentionally. For this commander in particular, his background did not give him a lot of opportunities to work with women. Unbeknownst to him though, he effectively isolated me and deeply hurt me. After a few days of being upset and calls and emails to numerous mentors, including my own commander who was in Germany at the time, I decided to confront him directly about the situation.

What he did absolutely violated equal opportunity policy. During our rotation, there were two males of the same rank (Captain) who were attached at the hip whenever possible. These two were roommates, went to the gym together, ate all meals together, etc. No one would ever question them, however because I am a female, I could not spend the same amount of time with a male of my same rank because of perception. What perceptions? The perception that we were cheating on our significant others? The perception that we were hiding secrets from others, including his spouse and my fiancé? The truth is that we disclosed everything with our other halves and upon return to the States, we all got to know each other even better.

These perceptions grew purely because we spent a lot of spare time together. I will point out that while others were going out on the weekends and drinking (legally) and going to clubs or bars, we would be the designated drivers every time. I acknowledge that (some) women and men alike can earn reputations because of certain behaviors or actions in the work place or in their free time; I am not one of those people and neither was my friend. I have never had an issue with upholding my reputation before in my life so why would it be an issue now? My work ethic and performance over the deployment did nothing to stop senior leaders in our unit from spreading rumors and taking action to "protect" this male lieutenant from "perception."

When I addressed the commander directly, I shared two main thoughts. First, when he told the first lieutenant to spend more time with his soldiers and less with us, he effectively isolated me with one other male with which to spend my time. Secondly, once he told his other Lieutenant not to spend time with me due to perception, he *completely* isolated me as a female officer in a foreign country. I had no other females that I could professionally vent to and now, I had no males of my same rank either. What was I supposed to do? Was I supposed to watch everyone else go out on the weekends while I stay in my room so that no one else has to be concerned about perception? Am I supposed to sit by myself at the dining facility? Or run circles around a Romanian base alone?

The commander and I talked it out, but I never felt the same with that unit. I felt betrayed. I felt that even though I put in an incredible amount of overtime and did duties that were much outside of my assigned responsibility, I was not treated as such. *I was just a part of a rumor mill; those leaders that I trusted did not stick up for me, support me, or try to stop the rumors. Instead, these leaders isolated me due to "perception."* If I could have left the military at that moment, I would have done so. Due to my military commitment however, I did not have that option.

Part II: Evaluation Season

A few months after our return from Romania, I had the opportunity to take a company Executive Officer (XO) job in a different battalion. During the time I spent as an XO, we capped at 220 personnel in the company. I changed commanders and then First Sergeants (1SG). We fired a First Sergeant and went without one for six months. Anyone who knows how essential a 1SG is in the "Top Three" can imagine the struggle. Despite these challenges and numerous others, I was proud of my performance and others recognized my abilities as well. Of course, I say that humbly, absolutely acknowledging that I accomplished nothing alone, but only with the help of my peers and subordinates.

After eleven months in this beyond stressful and demanding position, it was time for my OER. Overall, the OER comments were very strong. I was happy and absolutely satisfied; I felt that the evaluation perfectly captured the work I did for the company and my individual successes.

After the evaluation was complete, my Battalion Commander (my senior rater) invited me to discuss the details of his comments. Again, I had no issue with anything in the write-up; I was honored with the statements. I wish, however, that he would have never told me who he rated above me. Enumeration, or a numerical ranking against your peers, is essential on evaluations. I was ranked #2 of 8 with strong overall comments; again, no issues. Once my senior rater told me, however, who received the #1 spot, I was stunned and heartbroken.

The individual who received the higher rating held a position of much less responsibility and had only been in our company a few months. He was a great leader and very competent at his job, however it did not make sense to me that he was rated higher. I was the company XO that held a company of 220 soldiers together during a year of transition and he was the battalion medical officer, who supervised about 15 Soldiers. It did not make sense to our commander either who saw us both perform daily.

The difference? He was a prior service Ranger who had been in the Special Forces. I acknowledge that he had more experience and more qualifications. I also saw firsthand the differences in our jobs and performances over that period of time and did not agree that I should have taken the number two spot. I acknowledge that even on the civilian side of things, additional certifications and work experience could absolutely play a part in promotion and evaluation. However, I also believe that if it were between me and a woman with additional badges but decreased responsibility, I would have easily been #1. He was rated as having increased potential after only a few months in the unit because of the badges on his uniform and his male demeanor, not because of his *actual* abilities.

The same feelings grew in my chest again. Here I am, completing the most difficult eleven months so far in my life. I worked many early mornings and late nights. I had key personnel missing from my unit for months. In those times, I covered down and performed their duties. I stood in for my commander on countless occasions during her absences without fail (she survived breast cancer and lost her mother during this time). There is no doubt that I gave 110% of my energy to that job, only to be told that someone else who did not put in a quarter of the effort had more potential. I felt betrayed, let down, and most of all, I felt like I was treated differently because of my gender. If I had been a male and all else was equal, I would have received that top rating.

I did not address the battalion commander at this time, but my commander did. She stepped up for me and explained what I did not feel comfortable saying. He did not change the rating, but I hope that he learned to look at things differently in the future.

Part III: Evaluation Season… 12 Months Later

After that evaluation, an opportunity arose for a different job on a different base, about an hour away. I took the opportunity! For the next 12 months I again went above and beyond as the Battalion S4, working longer hours than most and performing at a maximum level. I saw our battalion through the brigade's conversion from an infantry brigade to an armored brigade, obviously a very supply intensive effort. We did well as a battalion in this effort and in many other projects during that year.

As evaluation season came around (today in fact), I got snubbed again. It is almost like déjà vu; my battalion commander, my senior rater, brought me in his office to show me the evaluation. Overall, I am incredibly pleased with the evaluation. The comments are strong, and my rating is in the highest category. Towards the end of the discussion, he unfortunately showed me the numbers and breakdown. On the evaluation I was listed #3 of 20; this is a fantastic position being as I am currently a promotable First Lieutenant serving in a Captain slot, meaning I am rated against other Captains. I was ecstatic about the numbers... until I found out who was immediately above me at #2.

The individual who holds the #2 spot has only been in the unit two weeks! I was and still am shell-shocked. How is someone who has performed at the top for twelve months rated lower to someone who has only been present for *two weeks?* He was so new; he could not even access a computer yet. Again, this male officer is prior service with combat arms experience. I absolutely believe that, if all else were equal, I could have retained the #2 spot; the difference between being in the top 10% and top 15% of your peers.

Again, for the third time in a short four years, I am watching months and months of work go down the drain. I am deflated. I feel that my early mornings and late nights made little to no difference in my evaluation. Most of all, the openness with which my battalion commander shared his logic is insulting. "I just like what he is doing already." Well, I think I should take notes. I need to figure out what magic qualities my male counterparts have that allow them to be consistently rated above me regardless of their decreased time in the unit and decreased responsibilities.

Conclusion

There are more situations outside of these that happen daily, weekly, etc. From someone walking into a conference room with women and men and referring to the group as "gents" ... to a young soldier having the phrase "no fat chicks allowed" written on the front glass of his car window. From someone referring to me as my husband's "chew toy" while speaking on *my own office phone* to a peer of mine... to a superior warning me that while visiting home for my high school reunion (while my husband was away at training), to be careful not to run into any complicated old high school boyfriends. Also, from being nominated to be a General's aide and being told I didn't get the job because I was a female... to reading leadership articles distributed by our superiors that use phrases like "leadership is based on the knowledge of men" and "man is the fundamental instrument of war." Of course, these discussions have context and detail and people do not always mean to be offensive. But ask me if I believe that gender inequality is real, and I will respond with a definitive "YES."

-- Afterword --

I write the next portion as an update. A day after the OER counseling, I asked to speak to my battalion commander. We shut the door and he invited me to share what was going on. I told him that the enumeration portion of my evaluation had been bothering me and if he was okay with it, I would like to tell him what I was feeling. He did not have to welcome this conversation, but he did- and we continued. I told him that I debated on waiting until the evaluation was final (just a few more days) before speaking to him, but I did not want to wait any longer. I told him that I did not want him to change the rating but that I did not understand how someone with only two weeks in the unit had already shown more potential than I did during a twelve-month period.

After I shared my thoughts, he responded. He told me that he knew he was wrong during the initial sit-down and later that day beat himself up about it. He offered to change the rating (I again tried to resist this with no success) and apologized. He told me that as a Lieutenant, he felt betrayed by a female commander who gave his female peer higher ratings. I thanked him for being approachable and suggested that it might be a better idea to ask people if they want to know who is rated above them. While he may personally prefer to know, I would prefer not to know. I do not work to compete with others or to obtain a certain rating; I work to do the best job I can.

What did I learn from this situation? I have reflected on the three situations I wrote about above (Romania, the first evaluation, and the second evaluation). I realize that in each situation, I took a slightly different approach. In Romania I chose to confront the situation directly. I was not abrasive nor was I disrespectful. I chose my words carefully and said the minimum of what I planned to say. During the first evaluation I mentioned, my commander was a strong, bold, and supportive influence. She stood up for me and had no problem saying _exactly_ what we both thought. When the battalion commander stood by his word, she stood by me. In this most recent scenario, I had the courage to have the real conversation. I said the words that I meant. I said that I believed gender played the biggest role in the enumeration. I have grown, and I now have courage that I did not have before.

Moving forward, I would like to share just a couple pieces

of advice with anyone reading. First, be who you are and be proud of it. Whether you are a woman, man, gay, straight, religious, atheist, soldier, civilian, or any combination or any other category. You must be proud of your dedication to your work, your country, your soldiers (or employees), and the mission. If you are honest to your word and set a foundation of honorable values, you cannot go wrong. Although you may not feel comfortable talking to your boss, or their boss, when issues arise, this courage will develop over time. Harvest it, do not discourage it. If I were in my boss's shoes, I would want honest feedback, too.

Next, be smart. *Be cognizant of your actions and the reputation you build. Be constantly aware of what people think and say, but never care too deeply or let on that you care at all.* Be who you are and be proud of it, just make sure that you are on the right track and going in the right direction. Find mentors, but not the formal ones. Picture yourself in a tough situation. Who do you call for advice? That is your mentor. Who is your second choice? Third? These are your mentors; stay in touch with them.

Often, we speak of "minorities" as being underrepresented and stereotyped. Being the member of a minority, however, gives an opportunity. Know and embrace the fact that our actions represent the whole. Whether it is gender, race, sexual orientation, etc. our actions can be extremely positive. In the past few years there has been an incredible amount of change in the world with the increasing empowerment of women and equal rights for those of any sexual orientation. As a minority, when we stand up for ourselves we are standing up for many others at the same time.

SHARON HEBERT, SGT
United States Air Force

I was born and raised on Air Force bases as my dad was a "lifer", so it made perfect sense when I made the decision to follow in his footsteps and enlist in the United States Air Force in 1978.

I saw many changes during my short 4 years on active duty such as:

1. When I went through Basic Training in San Antonio, the women were not allowed to fire a weapon nor go through the gas mask training, which was typical of the times. However, halfway through my enlistment this process changed, and women handled and fired weapons and were trained in proper gas mask procedures.
2. Women were discharged upon becoming pregnant, but halfway through my enlistment, women were given a choice to stay in or discharge. By the end of my time in the Air Force, it was no longer a choice as women stayed in to complete their commitment of their enlistment.
3. During Basic Training when our uniforms (solid olive-green color) were issued to us, we were given men's uniforms as they didn't have fatigues for women. The smallest waist size was 26" and the shirts were men's sizes also. We either had to alter them ourselves or find a good seamstress to ensure they were within the 35-10 regulation. We also had issues with the boots as they only had men's sizes. And forget about getting the required steel toed boots in a woman's size. I had small feet (size 6) and had to go to the Medical Group and receive a waiver to have the boots specially made for me in my size. The "doctor's" note stated in the block for medical condition, "Feet too small".

It took 8 months to receive my special order of steel toed boots. Again, around halfway through my enlistment, we finally received women's fatigues (permanent press, even), boots, etc.

4. From 1978 -1982, women were not allowed in combat as they are in today's military operations, unless it was behind the lines in the medical field(s), staff support, etc.

When I enlisted in 1978, the Air Force had just opened up maintenance jobs to females (a few, not all of them) and I was selected as a Non-Destructive Inspector (NDI). When I was assigned to my first permanent home station, Dyess AFB, Texas, I was the first female assigned there. We had one restroom in our shop and it said, "Men". My first order of business was to paint over the "Men" and I created a sign to hang that said, "Female Occupied". As women, we were trail blazers and mentors for those that came after us. We had to be perfect in every sense of the word and prove ourselves over and over again. I am proud to say I did my job in this sense and at 3 ½ years into my enlistment, was the first female awarded the Master Technician Badge in the Strategic Air Command (SAC). To this day, it's one of my proudest accomplishments as I helped pave the way for women to follow me and take up the torch.

While in the military, I was subjected to sexual harassment, discrimination and many forms of bullying, etc. However, I learned how to become one of the guys and let things bounce off of me that I wouldn't allow today. It was an unwritten rule that you didn't complain, or things would become much worse for you.

For example: I was sent TDY to Cold Lake Canada as one of our aircraft had crash landed and we were the recovery team. As usual, I was the only female on this team but did my job. It was freezing and snowing the day we had to go to the runway and jack, by hand, the aircraft to release the main landing gear that failed to deploy during the landing. The team spent 12 hours jacking and we had to do it in unison to maintain an even process and ensure it was level or we could have damaged components of the aircraft. Even though I was the only female on the team, and the only NDI technician, these guys knew my reputation for excellence and "never quit" attitude. No, I wasn't as strong as my male counterparts and couldn't go as long as they could, so they adjusted the times each team on each side would switch out. We determined the time by my team (2 people) and the other side's team going as long as we could which was approximately 15 minutes and that's what we did. Not one complaint from the guys that the time was shortened to accommodate me. They could have gone twice as long between switch-outs, but they understood my need to contribute to the team and allowed it to happen. This shows that even though I was able to gain the respect of most of the males I worked with, I was still vulnerable to an attack.

That evening, we all went out to dinner and we played some pool to unwind after working 14 hours straight. On our way back to the motel, the guys that usually escorted me to my room on the 2nd floor (they were very protective) saw my assistant NCOIC (Non-Commissioned Officer in Charge) was on the 2nd floor also and he would be escorting me. When we reached my room, he suddenly grabbed me in a bear hold and started kissing me. I could not move or get away. I was fighting him and finally he let me go. I rushed into my room and locked the door. I was shaken up badly but knew I couldn't say anything or lodge a complaint. This was an unspoken rule during my time in anyway. The next morning the NCOIC (our boss during this TDY) called me away from my work and took me to a private office. I knew what was coming but I kept my mouth shut. He had me sit down and he casually leaned against the desk (looming over me in a position of authority). He said that he wanted to talk about what happened the night before (I guess the assistant NCOIC had gone to him afraid). I looked at him and said I didn't know what he was talking about. He said, that's a good answer. He further went on to tell me that it was my word against the guy's word and I would be the loser if I went forward with any complaint; that my career would be destroyed, and I would not "survive" the fall out. I reiterated I had no idea what he was referring to. He said, good then, we understand each other and that was that. We left, and I never said a word, and I never received an apology from the much older TSgt for what he did.

As I think back on this horrible situation, I've often asked myself, would I make the same decision? And the answer is always yes, I would definitely make the same decision. If I would have lodged a complaint, I would have been ripped apart and my honorable career flushed down the toilet because that's the way things were then. I praise and thank God every day that I didn't actually get raped as that was a true blessing. In this time frame within the military, it was extremely more difficult if you were a pretty woman. The guys thought a pretty head was all we had to offer, and you were labeled either gay or dim witted, of which I am neither!

I was a young, naïve but extremely hardworking young girl, when I enlisted but my experiences, both good and bad, shaped me into the woman I am today. I have many good memories, also, of my time in the service. Through hard work and perseverance, I did gain the respect of my male counterparts, but there were always those that no matter how I performed, were never going to accept me.

For example (good experience): We had an inspection on a B-52 co-pilot's window. A male co-worker and I gathered up our equipment and headed over. The B-52 is a huge aircraft but the fuselage and backbone is skinny and narrow. Back in those days we didn't have fall protection equipment so when we arrived at the aircraft, my male counterpart asked me if I would do the inspection. I said sure, no problem. I knew something was off when he wouldn't help me drag the equipment onto the wing for access to the fuselage, but again, I didn't say anything. What I had to do was place my inspection materials into a small toolbox type container, then walk onto the curved and skinny/narrow fuselage towards the nose of the aircraft where the co-pilot's window was. I started walking like you would see a tightrope acrobat do in the circus and it was precarious to say the least. I came to a point where I could no longer thread my way through on my feet and had to sit down and straddle the fuselage as I scooted myself forward. By this point in the process, I had quite the crowd down below and they started cat calling and yelling things at me. That's when my co-worker (who was a huge bear of a guy) yelled at everyone to shut up and suddenly, the entire hangar was dead silent. The easy part was actually getting to the inspection site as I now had to lie prone and lean over the very end of the aircraft (nose) to gain access to perform the inspection. How I kept from slipping or falling off is by the grace of God. When I returned to the floor, my co-worker and I gathered our stuff up and began walking back to our shop. I didn't say anything (again, the law of the jungle) about why he wasn't helping me as I had figured it out, but he was praising my performance, and that's when he told me of his fear of heights. I told him, it was okay; we are all afraid of something and not to worry, I would never say a word to our other co workers and I've kept my word to this day. From this day forward, I had his complete respect and he became one of my fiercest protectors and champions. If you're reading this (you know who you are), thank you for always having my back and treating me as an equal with respect.

Another example (with both a good and a bad experience): We had a B-52 on our alert pad with an issue on the Wing Tip Gears (Outriggers). With equipment in hand, I went to the alert pad, where there was a crowd of high-ranking officials. This was a major issue as the alert pad aircraft were for our national security and highly critical to maintain serviceability at all times. Again, the access area was in a precarious position. The wing tip gear is what was used to stabilize the aircraft when fully fueled to capacity and we had a suspected crack on the right side. To make a long story short, gaining access to the area was extremely difficult and determining whether the crack existed or not was almost impossible due to the location. I had the Chief of Quality Inspection with me and he became my assistant. I performed the inspection 3 times to ensure the crack was truly there and then gave my determination. Our Base Commander, though professional, did not trust my determination and judgement. Even though he could have directed a 9-level to override my decision, and even though he tried to intimidate me into not recording the issue and placing a Red X in the aircraft forms, he was smart enough to know if there was a crack it could have meant his career. My Shop Chief and Assistant Shop Chief were called out to the aircraft and they could not see what I had seen, but also decided not to overturn my Red X determination. The Assistant NCOIC began bullying me and talking down to me, but that was not a surprise as he had never accepted me. However, my Shop Chief only asked me once if I was sure because if I wasn't, then it could mean bad news for me. When I said yes, he said okay then. The Quality Chief knew my work and completely supported my finding(s). Due to my determination, the wheel gear was removed and replaced with a defect-free one. That process took around 20-24 hours to complete and make the aircraft air worthy. This meant the aircraft was non-operational for approximately 24 hours. This was extremely bad as it was an alert pad aircraft.

What happened next would not have happened if the inspector that Red X'd an item in the forms had been a male! Once the gear was removed, the component that was possibly cracked (the Base Commander's words, not mine as I knew it was cracked) was taken to the NDI shop for further evaluation. Normally, the cracked item would be red tagged and turned in for disposal. Once it arrived in the shop, the Shop Chief and his Assistant began the inspection process and the Assistant Chief kept telling me that my career was over when and if it was proven that the component was not cracked.

It was awful listening to what he said to me. I was calm though as I was certain the crack existed. Additionally, the shop was crowded with high ranking individuals, including my Base Commander, and we all waited for the inspection findings to be revealed. Finally, my Shop Chief came out and started talking about my capabilities, dedication to duty, etc. and revealed that the crack was there, and I saved an aircraft and the crew from potential loss. He further stated that when he looked at it on the aircraft, he couldn't see what I had seen and that further proved how exceptional I was as an inspector.

The final thing he said made my heart swell with pride. He said that even if it hadn't been cracked, my duty to the crew, potential loss on the ground from a crash, safety and integrity of the aircraft were worth a wrong determination. The assistant Shop Chief very quickly changed his tune as he began talking about how he trained me, how he made me the inspector that I was, etc. It was totally laughable as I think back on it.

I have many more examples of disparate treatment and some other horror stories, but maybe in volume 2 of this great book I will be able to relate them.

In closing, I am proud of the 4 years I spent defending our great nation and would do it all again for this incredible opportunity. I am proud to have been a trailblazer and one of the many incredible military women that paved the way to today's military forces filled with remarkable and brave women. What an honor to have served and served faithfully.

SUNNY GUERIN, S. SGT.
UNITED STATES ARMY

I want to make it clear in the beginning that this is my perspective and I did not add names of other people in here, as I did not get any permission to use them.

I joined the Army in 2003 in a wild attempt to run away from a chaotic life that I had created. I was working in a small village in Alaska when I saw an ad for the Army on the computer. I decided that I would try to contact them and see what would come of it.

A recruiter from the Fairbanks office called me and began asking me a ton of questions; some were completely inappropriate. He wanted to know if I had piercings, and if so, where. When I told him I had a tongue piercing, he wanted to hear it click against my teeth through the phone. What a weirdo.

Anyhow, I scheduled a time to travel to Fairbanks to see the recruiter in November of 2003. A few days before I was supposed to leave, an elder from a nearby village passed away so I drove my snow machine sixty miles up the trail to go to the funeral. I decided to drive back home to Fort Yukon the morning that I was supposed to fly to Fairbanks. I left really early to hit the trail and was about fifteen miles out of town when the belt on my snow machine broke. I knew that there was no way I was going to make that plane if I didn't get moving. I started walking. It was around noon and the plane was supposed to land around 2:00 pm. I walked for about an hour before I heard another snow machine coming up the trail. Fortunately, another person decided to come back home the same day as I did, so I was able to catch a ride into town. I was sweating up a storm, after having ridden half the morning on a trail. I made it to the airstrip just as the plane was landing.

When I got to Fairbanks I went straight to the recruiting office. The guy there was a complete douche bag. He kept making weird sexual remarks, which were completely uncalled for, but at the time I did not understand the implications of that. He asked if I wanted to do hometown recruiting when I was done with basic and I could fly home and hand out flyers. I said sure.

Going to MEPS was interesting. I had tested pretty high on the ASVAB so I was able to select what I wanted to do. I told the guy I wanted to be a medic and I wanted to go overseas somewhere--I didn't care where at this point, I just wanted to go far away.

He asked what I thought about Germany and I said that sounded good. He said all I had to do was sign the paper, so I signed my name then was sworn in. I was in the Delayed Entry Program and selected a time to go to basic training in March of 2004.

I was off on another adventure to another village way downriver on the Yukon when it came time for me to leave for the Army. I drove down with friends, but due to the weather hitting -55 degrees, it was almost impossible to travel back home via snow machine. I ended up jumping on a plane to fly to Fairbanks with hardly a pair of clothes in my backpack when I took off to basic training.

BASIC TRAINING:

Basic was a new experience for me. I was always pretty outdoorsy, used to hard work, and--quite honestly--used to someone hollering at me. What I was not used to, was the heat of South Carolina and a bunch of women.

The first day they loaded us on the bus with our duffle bags full of army-issued equipment and whatever other bags we'd decided to bring with us. Fortunately, I only had a small backpack...BUT, I was in the back of the bus. The bus stopped and on stepped a couple of drill sergeants who began screaming something to the effect of "GET OFF THE FUCKING BUS!" Instantly people started to panic and rush off the dang bus. Now, when I say panic, these knuckleheads were climbing over people who could not move fast enough. I helped a few people get out of the bus aisle and get their stuff off of the bus. I was thinking to myself that these people have got to be crazy!

When I finally get off the bus, the drill sergeants have everyone lined up in formation. Well, at the time, I didn't know what the heck it was. They were screaming at us to get our bags and hold them above our heads. So as this panic-stricken group of people was holding bags above their heads, some people instantly started crying and put their bags down. The drill sergeants got in their faces and started screaming at them to hold the bags up. I think they quit on the spot or got kicked out. I have a strange response to stress: I find it funny and smile or laugh.

So, there was this whole group of people freaking out holding bags above their heads, drill sergeants screaming at them, and I start to chuckle. The moment I cracked a smile a drill sergeant homed in on me. He started yelling at me "What the fuck do you find so funny PRIVATE?!?"

And with a HUGE smile I yell "Nothing, Drill Sergeant!" He looks at me and says, "Then wipe that smile off your damn face!" Still smiling, I can't.

The majority of my basic training involved scrubbing tile (I am an expert!) and waxing floors, getting "smoked" because I couldn't keep the smile off my face, and complaining about the people who went to Sunday church to sleep and get out of cleaning.

I was also the person who ran back to the bay to make sure everyone's crap was lined up so that the barracks didn't get tossed into the middle of the floor, and we'd end up spending the night trying to put it all back together.

While I was at basic training I had a few funny friends that would send me a letter almost every day and I would have to do pushups for every letter I got...totally not funny.

Germany:

My first duty station was 485th CSB out of Hanau, Germany. I vaguely remember in-processing. I got to Pioneer Kaserne on Labor Day weekend. I was a mechanic reporting to my unit for the first time. My Platoon Sergeant picked me up, and he was a little bit more than surprised to find out that I was a woman. Due to the long weekend, they had already set me up in the men's barracks based on their thinking that Mechanic PVT "Sunny Mahler" was a male. I was bunked next to a man for the long weekend.

My first day to the formation was a new experience. I was not sure what to expect. Before formation I heard a knock on my door and another soldier was standing there. He was holding something out to me, saying it was the unit crest for my beret. I noticed that it was NOT a unit crest and was actually a branch insignia...I thought he was trying to fool me. He introduced himself as Jon, and little did I know that a few years down the road we would be married with children.

Jon and I decided we would get married on a whim in July of 2005. We were scheduled to deploy and both of us had leave, going home where we would let our families know what we were doing; Jon went to Ohio and I went to Alaska. A few weeks later we would meet back up in Germany and run off to Denmark and tie the knot.

Prior to deploying, our unit got a new battalion commander. She was an embarrassment to women in the military. She literally threw fits if things weren't her way and it made me sick to see how weak she was, in command of a battalion going into combat.

A few months later, on Halloween night to be exact, we were scheduled to deploy to Iraq. We packed up our things and headed out. Our first week we spent in Kuwait where we did a few trainings and went to the range and generally acclimatized.

It was a mess there: everyone was on edge, and the command team was kind of crazy and generally stressed. We were getting punished for the stupidest things. For example, we were securing our gear after a formation where they were inspecting all our gear. While I was packing my gear back to my tent, my pro-mask fell out. The First Sergeant saw me drop it and he picked it up and gave it to my squad leader with specific orders to "smoke" me for a couple hours in it. I had to put my pro-mask on in 100+ degree weather, in full combat gear, and do push-ups, flutter kicks, and front-back-go. I was never so pissed in my life. I was pretty much soaking wet with sweat and about dead by the time we were done, but it did nothing to quench the anger that had started burning. This would not be the end of my mishaps...Mishap is my middle name.

We ended up at Talil Air Base, where we conducted convoy operations and humanitarian missions. Somewhere between my getting smoked and going to Talil, my squad leader had disappeared. I don't remember what happened to him, but he had some issues and went home or something--I am not sure. The other mechanic and I held things together.

We installed beefed-up suspensions on all the Humvees in the unit; the equipment we had inherited from the previous unit was pretty beat up and needed to get up-armored for convoys. We started scheduling one at a time for armoring, and when we got them back, we noticed that the clearance in the wheel well was pretty nonexistent. We ended up having to order heavy-duty suspension kits and upgrade the suspensions.

We were getting the vehicles ready for a convoy in which the battalion commander wanted to tag along. We only had the windows and the sides of the Humvees with up armor at this time. The tops were either canvas tops or little hard tops (not up armor though). The battalion commander's vehicle happened to have the canvas top. When she noticed this, she jumped up and down screaming, over and over: "I will not go out the gate in a soft-top Humvee!" This was the most embarrassing example I had ever seen from a soldier. Even more embarrassing was how people catered to her. At any rate, they ended up taking a hard-top Humvee from a soldier and swapped her vehicle. What the hell? I was so disappointed. At that moment I made a promise to myself that as I climbed the ranks, I would never make my soldiers do something that I was not willing to do myself.

One fine day we had a rare event; we had company formation at the headquarters where I seldom went. The motor pool was out at the edge of the base where the Italians blew shit up, and we generally worked night shifts to keep out of the hot sun. We headed to the formation and I had to use the bathroom. I had one of my "battle buddies" come so she could keep an eye on my gear while I went in the stall. The bathrooms had very little room to move, so I left my flak jacket and weapon leaning outside the door where my buddy could watch it. Well, while I was using the bathroom, the battalion commander came in and asked my battle buddy if the weapon was hers. She said "No, ma'am." I piped up and said that it was mine; the commander said, "Well you can find me, as I have your unsecured weapon," and she proceeded to take my weapon into the Tactical Operations Center where officers were having a big briefing. Man, I pulled my pants up so damn fast and went running after her. She would not turn around. When she got to the TOC, the Sergeant at the door would not let me in, even when I told him that she had my weapon. Man, that was the shittiest day ever. I ended up standing in front of the Commander getting an Article 15 as well as being put on extra duty.

In the damn desert they had me reporting to work for a full day, then going to the headquarters at night until 11pm to sweep sand out of the desert and dig up palm trees and plant them in front of the headquarters. All the trees we dug up and planted eventually died. It was like a small victory for me! It was the stupidest thing I ever did. Now, this is when I made the second promise to myself. I was going to get my feet under me. I put my nose to my work and paid no attention to anything but my work.

I told my Sergeant that I wanted to compete for Soldier of the Month. He was surprised, but he supported me and said that he would send me. I studied my ass off for a month on Army regulations and combat drills, I worked out and I went to the armory every day to learn more about the SAW and .50 Cal, which we would have to operate during the competition.

I won Soldier of the Month, then I went to compete at a higher level and won Soldier of the Quarter. I went to compete at the brigade level and I lost to someone who had a "300" on their PT test. My Sergeant Major was not happy and thought they fluffed the paperwork. They had another competition. At this one we started with a PT test, went to the range and had to effectively operate three weapons. After that, we went to the brigade headquarters and had to go before the board. I was pretty exhausted at this point. In the end I had tied with the same soldier who beat me previously. In order to determine who would win, we had to recite the NCO Creed. He could not remember the whole thing. I smiled inside because I had that creed on the tip of my tongue! I was about to bellow it out when a bomb hit right outside the building. The sirens went off. I put on my gear and looked at the Sergeant Major, determined that I would win, and asked if I should continue. He smiled and said, "Carry on." There I was, reciting the NCO Creed, with sirens blaring in the background. I won that competition.

Towards the last few months of our deployment, we had TCNs (third-country nationals) working behind our motor pool, putting in a concrete pad. One of the companies under our battalion was responsible for guarding the TCNs and ensuring they were in line. Well, that company's convoy was hit, and they lost a couple soldiers, so their unit had a debriefing. Since we were the only soldiers out in the area, another of the female soldiers in my squad and I went to guard the TCNs. These little assholes had no respect for us because we were women. The moment we took guard they started lying around and stopped working. Then they would get all shifty and try to get out of sight. I had the interpreter tell them that they all needed to stay in the area where we could see them. One of the TCNs was allowed to have a little knife to rip open the cement bags. He stood up and started making obscene gestures and thrusting his hips towards us. He then grabbed the knife and looked at us and made a throat-cutting motion.

I put my gun to his face and screamed at him to lie face down. I radioed the First Sergeant and he came barreling out. We escorted the men off post and barred that guy from coming back on for work.

A few months into deployment, I got a Red Cross message that my grandmother was dying. I was not allowed to go home for her funeral because she was not considered a close enough family member, so they sent me to Qatar for a four-day "R&R" to unwind. The planes ended up being delayed and overbooked, so other soldiers and I were there for about eight days, which was a nice little break.

Back at Talil we kept getting bombed, and they were coming closer to where we were in the motor pool. At one point we were working on one of the trucks and as we heard a bomb hit, a spray of rocks came flying into our motor pool. We just jumped in one of the up-armored trucks to get cover. We decided that we would get sand bags to build up around the walls to add some protection from debris and shrapnel.

We had just pulled up with the LMTV loaded with sandbags, and I was dismounting, when another bomb hit. It was enough to cause the 600 lb. up-armored door to swing shut on me as I was getting out. I reached my hand across my chest to keep if from hitting me and I felt my entire bone shove straight out the back of my shoulder socket. I hollered for the other mechanic to come help me. I told him to try putting my shoulder back into place; he couldn't. I reached back with my other hand and hit it until I felt it pop back into place. I instantly felt better. I lit a cigarette and waited for the all-clear signal. My shoulder felt weird, but I figured it would be okay; that is, until I went to put my soft cap on and my arm fell out of joint. I hollered for help again and was told I needed to go to the hospital.

They wanted to medevac me to Landstuhl, Germany. I begged them not to since my unit was to redeploy in a week. They made me put my arm in an immobilizer until I returned to Germany. In hindsight, I should have let them medevac me at the time and get my arm fixed.

When we redeployed back to Germany, I had a few medical appointments before I took leave. We had a month of leave after deployment, so I decided it was time for my husband to meet my family. We needed at least thirty days to get to the village where I live by plane, then by taking a snow machine to our home 160 miles up the river.

When we returned back to Germany, it was announced that our unit was disbanding in the next few months and the Kaserne was to be turned over to the Germans. We were all waiting for orders to where we would go next. My husband and I got orders for 101st Airborne; we were to report in April.

Meanwhile, we were tasked with cleaning out the basements of our barracks, which were old WWII buildings. Three of us were in the basement handing boxes of old documents out and it was dusty and dank down there. We also found dead birds. There was something in this space that was not right. We started coughing, I had a hard time breathing and crawled out one of the windows. My whole chest and neck was red. One of the other guys was coughing so hard he broke ribs; the other had to inject himself with an EpiPen.

The next day we went on a company run and as we went by the buildings, I started having a hard time breathing/ Next thing you know, I woke up in an ambulance on my way to a German hospital. They injected me with some substance, and I felt better. After this I had odd health problems.

Before I left Germany, I went before the E-5 board and got promoted to Sergeant. A few weeks later I found out I was pregnant right before I was to PCS (Permanent Change of Station) to Fort Campbell. Because of all this, my husband and I decided to buy a house in Tennessee sight unseen. Oh, my goodness! The decisions we made that could have ended badly but worked out in the end.

When I reported to my unit at 101st DSTB they were a little less than pleased that I was pregnant. We were scheduled to deploy in January and I was supposed to have my baby in November. My husband was reclassified so he was in training the whole summer, then he returned in September and was scheduled for another training for a month. He came home in October, and I had our baby on November 7th after almost dying under the horrendous care of the Army hospital. My husband deployed to Afghanistan a month later, right before Christmas.

After I had my son I had 30 days of medical leave. I was not cleared by my doctor to return to physical activity at this point. I reported to formation and my First Sergeant demanded that I participate in a company run. I was still healing from a c-section and was experiencing post-delivery bleeding after a very hard birth. He was yelling at me saying I needed to be in shape to deploy in a month. So I ran. When we got back from the run my company commander wanted to see me. He asked if I had a Family Care Plan for someone to take my month-and-a-half-old baby for a year while I deployed. I told him that I did not have anyone that would be able to care for my child at the time. My parents lived on a trapline in the middle of the wilderness in Alaska and my in-laws were not able to care for him either. He said, "Then I will process paperwork to chapter you out of the military."

I was stunned at what I was hearing. I just had my baby two months ago, you want me to deploy for a year, his dad is already deployed, and because I have no one to watch him you won't work with me.

I asked to be on a different deployment schedule than

my husband; perhaps we could switch units or something. They wouldn't hear of it. They began paperwork that day and even had a thank you for your service award typed up. I was pissed. I had three years left on my contract and I was not taking this lying down.

I used my anger to fuel an emotionally charged letter to Marcy Kaptor, who was my husband's representative, and filed a congressional complaint against my unit. They called me in the office the next day and asked me if I could do a PT test. Even though I was still not cleared by my doctor to do a PT test, I did one anyway to prove a point. I passed: that was all that mattered. They were told to find me a non-deploying unit.

They sent me over to the 101st NCO Academy to interview. I think they expected me to fail under the pressure. Little did they know that I thrive under pressure. I interviewed with the Sergeant Major and he told me to report to the WLC (Warrior Leader Course) chief the next week.

My experience then went from watching the worst leadership I had seen, to working alongside some of the best leaders the Army had to offer. I ran the operations, went to the E-6 board, and was promotable for the longest time. I went to the instructors' course and eventually worked as a WLC instructor.

While I was at the Academy, I got a call from the Red Cross that said my dad had cancer and he had a maximum of thirty days to live. Apparently, he had been sick for a long time and my mom had finally called someone to fly out to our cabin to take him to the hospital. My mom was still out at our cabin in the woods;

Resilient Warriors

I knew I could not tell her, so I told her to call dad.

Then I worked to get a bush pilot to fly out to pick her and my sister up from the cabin, so they could be in town. My world was crushed. The same month my dad passed away, I made points and was promoted to E-6 Staff Sergeant. It was such a bittersweet moment because I would call him every chance I got, and I could hear the pride in his voice when I would tell him that I was promotable. I just wanted to tell him that I made SSG and hear him one last time.

During my time at the NCO Academy, my husband was deployed a couple more times. Each time he came back changed a little more. PTSD hung heavy in our relationship and we knew that if we stayed in the Army any longer, we would not survive it married. Our ETS (Expiration of Term of Service) date was April of 2011.

Right before I was to get out of the Army, they scheduled me for a surgery on my shoulder, in 2010. Four days after the surgery, I found out I was pregnant with our second child. This was a very stressful time for us. My husband had just got back from deployment in October, I had found out I was pregnant in November, and we were about to ETS in April. We decided that we would go to Alaska, closer to my family.

We struggled to keep our heads above water for the first couple of years. We had attempted to make different things work in different places. PTSD already strained our relationship, we had financial problems, and I ended up with a myriad of medical issues that I am still fighting in the VA appeals process.

It has been an honor to serve and it has changed my life drastically. I cannot say much for the care after you leave the military. I had no support system, no information, and little help to deal with the third aspect of our relationship now: Post-Traumatic Stress Disorder. It impacts everything from family dynamics to going to the grocery store.

We have tried different group therapies and it feels like instead of having someone who truly understands what you are going through, they have a student who is studying as your lifeline, and they are reading a script from a book. It's sad. Really sad. Thankfully, we have learned to manage and build on our strengths as a family and get through all of this together. We are still married and who knows what life will toss our way. Whatever it is, I am sure we can handle it.

TRISH RUSSELL, CAPTAIN
UNITED STATES AIR FORCE

As a third-generation female entering the military, I thought I knew what I was getting into. Growing up in a military home the core values were drilled into our heads and held up as a measure for our actions. I lived a life with rules that made right and wrong clear and simple, even black and white. It was not until I joined active duty service did I begin to realize there is nothing simple about right and wrong during times of war.

Military Training

September 11, 2001, I sat with my history professor reviewing the most recent paper I wrote for Western Civilization. We heard over the radio about planes crashing into towers; however, I assumed it had something to do with prop planes and an inexperienced pilot causing a disaster. When I returned to my freshman dorm I soon realized my mistake. Since all classes were cancelled that day there was plenty of time to watch the news on a friend's television and absorb the knowledge we were going to war.

Only a few weeks before, I had signed the dotted line to serve my country after graduation. I was a Reserve Officer Training Corps cadet on a four-year scholarship. Even with the news of our country being attacked it never occurred to me to change my mind and find a way to get out of my commitment. Growing up with the military's core values as my moral compass it felt like the right thing to do. Even with four years of military training during wartime I was naïve to what awaited me on the other side of graduation.

Part of the naivety may come from the fact for me it was

simple. I committed, I was in. My environment probably also played a big role, I lived in a bubble. Attending a liberal arts college as the only military cadet was an interesting experience. I remember my sophomore year when we entered Iraq. My roommate and I watched on television as the bombing started. I was ironing my ROTC uniform in the room we shared and above her bed was a "Don't Invade Iraq" sign. Even in that polarized situation it never occurred to me to walk away. Our family served for generations, women and men, you could say it's the family business.

Even though our cadre prepared us as best they could for joining the military during war time, I believe it's safe to say I lived in a sheltered environment. Reality didn't begin to set in until technical training, where I learned how to perform my duties as an Intelligence Officer. It wouldn't take long for the veil to fully fall from my eyes.

Military Service

Fall of 2008, three short years after commissioning into the United States Air Force, I was off to my second deployment. This time I was to join the United States Army as an augmentee, which simply means I was taken out of my specialty to fill whatever job was needed in the war zone. By this time the Army needed extra bodies and other branches were doing their best to support the ground war. While it was unnerving and slightly annoying, you had no idea what job you would be expected to perform, it made sense. We were at war and we were in the fight together. Still a very simple and clear outlook on the world due to my moral compass.

Even with my patriotic attitude and naïve view of right

and wrong, I was still surprised they trusted me with grenades and guns. When you sign up for a desk job with a branch of the military everyone says is "soft and more civilian than military", the last thing you expect is to be dropped in the desert with a rifle and canteen. I half wondered if they had lost their mind giving me weapons; however, women apparently have a knack for rifles and I qualified as a sharpshooter. While that helped me feel confident I wouldn't shoot my foot off, I worried about some of my counterparts. We had three months to become soldiers and I prayed we had figured it out. Fortunately, it was not the Army's first rodeo with augmentees and most were assigned to jobs they were able to perform.

When we landed in Afghanistan my childhood of learning right from wrong was shattered. I quickly discovered the true complexity of war time. Even with my reality shattering around me, skewing my lens of right and wrong, no longer knowing up from down, I was all in.

I was all in because freshman year of college, only weeks after signing on the dotted line, terrorists killed Americans on our soil with our resources. Even though I did not understand the actual cost of war, I was committed to figuring it out. And I knew just enough to be dangerous, like an 18-year-old with a license. An 18-year-old has had enough training to maneuver through a standardized test, hours behind the wheel to get from home to school to work; however, not enough experience behind the wheel to respond correctly when you start hydroplaning.

That was me. 3 years of active duty experience and one deployment under my belt, plopped in a combat zone, told to be a soldier and given a job I never heard of. And I was just like that 18-year-old. I had enough training and practice to say, "Yes, I got this! I can handle life and death situations every single day."

Over the next 7 months I manned an operations desk providing support and threat analysis to assist our troops during real time operations. While I had never heard of the job, my intelligence training proved helpful and my 3 months of combat training gave me a basic awareness of the situation. As my world forever changed I discovered some interesting things:

- Peeing in a water bottle while wearing battle equipment is just as hard as it sounds.
- A sweet, kind, Jesus loving gal can learn to curse just as well as a sailor.
- Night terrors really can cause you to wake up your roommate.
- Bread and water is not a punishment. Sometimes it's a gift to the digestive system.
- Toby Keith is great in concert.
- It only takes a few months to question what is right and what is wrong.

When my time serving the Army came to an end I was sent back to my unit. The same body returned but the mind inside had forever changed. Some of the noticeable changes were how I spent my time. A typical day for me began with staring at a wall, eating, working hard, staring at a wall, going to bed, hours of nightmares, then it would start all over again. I had no idea my routine was unusual. Fortunately, those around me did know and took the time to reach me.

My mother consistently nagged me to get help, God love her, but I tuned her out. Luckily, she wasn't the only one who noticed a change in my behavior. One day, out of the blue, a previous mentor of mine asked to get lunch and spoke the words that forever changed my life. "Ms. March is concerned about you. Are you sure you're ok?" It took someone I respected deeply, who saw me on a regular basis, to show concern for me, to shake me out of my new normal and wake up. The conversation really rattled me, it also brought my mom's deep concern, gentle nudges, and constant support to mind. The next week I began the terrible process of seeking help.

The conversation that day was the first step on my 10-year journey of accepting my new normal and since then I fight to design it. I wonder if my life would be as it is if Ms. March had not spoken with my mentor. And then if my mentor had not made the time in her crazy schedule to lovingly, openly have "a talk" with me. I'm forever thankful to them.

As I began the mental health journey it quickly became evident that my life had to change, or I would not be able to be a part of society. I battled suicidal thoughts. I desired self-sabotage. I hated the comforts and niceties of life, I longed for war. I understood combat but not much else.

I chose to leave the military because my ability to transition between my job and civilian life was tenuous at best. If I ever wanted to have a family I worried about my ability to be a mother while deploying every six months. Even when the war ended, I worried about who I would be then, now understanding the complexities of war. While my diagnosis with Post Traumatic Stress

Disorder led to my decision to leave, what came next surprised me.

After the Military

When my letter arrived in the mail stating I was 70% disabled due to PTSD, I felt as if the world around me was falling apart. Disabled? Me? I wasn't broken. I came home with all my body parts, there was no way I could be disabled. As I fought this declaration over my life I started to discover maybe I was...

During my exit interview, I shared with the therapist how I coped with the world around me. No news, unless for work. No crowds. Limited to no contact with new people. Constant nightmares (I viewed as memories). Inability to care about other's daily struggle. Deep rooted mistrust – self-preservation attitude. Low tolerance for someone having a bad day. Limited meal variations, same 3 or 4 meals each day. No physical touch with family. Only conversation or topic that felt safe was current operations or sharing previous war stories.

I was truly dumbfounded when I received a 70% disabled verdict. For 6 months I'd worked hard to talk to people about their children and family situations. I was trying to care about someone else's relationship struggles. I was going to counseling, identifying triggers, and accepting there was a world outside of the combat zone. Granted, I regularly had to ask myself, "How would a normal person respond in this situation?" so I didn't respond instinctively and make people uncomfortable (again). My efforts had grown leaps and bounds from when I first came home. I went to a baby shower and laughed. On top of all those efforts I made a very difficult decision. I chose to leave the military because I had an awareness to the level of my PTSD. All these purposeful steps led me to believe I was well on the way to recovery!!! While I was certainly on the road to recovery, there was a lot more to healing than I realized.

I lived in a constant state of fear. Fear of lashing out on my family. Fear of hurting myself. Fear of saying the wrong thing in a social situation, yet again. Fear of...many things.

I'll never be "all better" or "fixed." Instead, I've come to accept I will live in a new normal. What I can tell you with certainty is today I have strong tools to help me cope and respond to the world around me. I'm able to mentally and emotionally process relationships, expectations, hopes and dreams. Not perfectly but a lot healthier than before. For 7 years I believed I would always "be this way" and there was no cure. Then one day I decided there had to be a way. I wanted to watch the fireworks with my kids. It was important for my children to experience amusement parks, football or baseball games, and friendships. If I couldn't do this for myself, how in the world was I going to show my children?

My first step was to desire something different. I was tired of living in a box and sheltering myself from the outside world. It's one thing to choose who to interact with and which friendships to nurture. For those with PTSD we live in a mental prison waiting for the next breakdown or nightmare, which can be very unpredictable. My husband coming home and sharing about a hard day at work would trigger nightmares and send my anxiety through the roof.

As I declared my wish for a different life, I have to admit, there was not a lot of hope inside. I'd been through therapy. Many times. I always outgrew my therapists and the last one was not encouraging about my ability to watch war movies or historical documentaries with my husband. So, I continued to want and wish but thought maybe I was asking for too much.

I had a family. 3 beautiful children. A loving husband. Parents and sister who care for me. That's enough. They know my disability and accept me for who I am. Was more even possible?

Yes. It is. If you are craving more outside of your PTSD, current life situation, I want you to know it is VERY possible.

My first step in a 3-year process was a choice. I had to choose to believe in something greater than myself. Whether a charity, faith system, future possibility, I had to get outside of my head. Even as I took this initial step I battled with doubt, insecurity, hateful self-talk, survivor's guilt, and flashbacks.

Some truths about reintegration I discovered:

- It's difficult to find a quality company
- Job skills didn't translate
- The culture was very different
- Loss of mission and purpose

I was exhausted mentally and emotionally, longing for something more. **I needed so much more for my life. As a survivor there had to be more.** My first steps to reintegrate:

1. **Say YES** when someone who cares for you suggests trying something new --- I was so deep in my head I couldn't see the world around me accurately. There were 3 times in my journey saying "yes" changed the trajectory of my life and they led to unlocking my brain again.

2. **Build your OWN support team.** Either invite one or two loved ones in to your journey or a combination of a loved one and new friends. Tell them when you're having difficult days, share the moments of celebration, and try your best to not put up walls. I have boundaries with the rest of the world but there are a handful of people who have full access to my head and heart. They have *earned* this trust through years of friendship and decades of family ties. Starting with one or two people will be a paradigm shift, we become vulnerable again and emotions are brought to the surface we may prefer to keep locked away.

3. **Take responsibility for my actions & future**. This step was really difficult and continues to be a process. It involves my thought patterns, how I design my days, the way I treat my loved ones, show up to my profession, so many aspects to taking ownership of our lives. The step that catapulted me on this journey was going to work for a team I believed in and trusting them. Some really bad-hard decisions were made by higher leadership; however, I never lost faith in the team I served on. That reminded me a lot of the military, so I was able to embrace the ups and downs of the job, which helped my brain and emotions to integrate into the civilian world for

the first time since being in the military. This was my 4th job in the civilian world and while I performed well at the previous 3 they were not positive work environments and my brain was unable to adapt. I believe **a critical piece for my reintegration was taking responsibility for my thoughts and actions AND joining a team I could trust.**

I'll leave you with the first steps to my reintegration process. They took 3 years and can be quite overwhelming in the beginning. ***Who am I kidding, they can still be a lot to process!!*** Our brains are never the same after trauma and we shouldn't try to make them "as they were." We have a new way of seeing people and situations. Let's continue exploring it and unlock our own lens to view the world around us.

Made in the USA
Columbia, SC
31 July 2018